THE PRIMARY GOAL OF THE ATLAN
SUPPORT SUSTAINABLE GROWTH, h
SECURITY IN THE ATLANTIC HEMISPHERE.

As Eminent Persons of our Hemisphere, we are united in our drive to build a dynamic and harmonious Atlantic Community by championing free and open trade and investment, promoting access for all to affordable energy, accelerating human development, encouraging economic, educational and technical cooperation, respecting human dignity and enhancing human security, facilitating a favorable business environment, generating sustainable and inclusive growth and development, and cultivating a culture of lawfulness across our four continents. Through our activities we seek to turn policy goals into concrete results and agreements into tangible benefits. We seek to advance our cooperation by engaging those with shared values as well as interests, and in being primarily non-governmental, less constrained by official positions.

We offer our Initiative as a place where sound politics and technical solutions can productively intersect, and where our members can bring their personal influence to bear in realizing solutions and opportunities. We invite the cooperation and participation of the private sector, labor, political parties, academic institutions and other non-governmental actors and organizations in both our national and regional efforts.

A NEW **ATLANTIC COMMUNITY**

Generating Growth, Human Development and Security in the Atlantic Hemisphere

A DECLARATION AND CALL TO ACTION

BY THE EMINENT PERSONS OF THE ATLANTIC BASIN INITIATIVE

Today, Atlantic peoples are connecting as never before. We are bound together by growing flows of energy, goods and services; possibilities afforded by education, technology, infrastructure and investment; and the scourges of crime, violence, human trafficking and drugs. Our diverse societies are benefiting from greater access to each other's markets, resources, and talent. But even as growing Atlantic interdependencies spawn new opportunities, they are also generating new vulnerabilities along the interrelated arteries upon which our societies depend.

Together we have an opportunity to build a new foundation of cooperation for the Atlantic Basin that harnesses the dynamism of our diverse societies to provide greater access to secure energy, generate sustainable and inclusive growth, and promote human development and security—not only in the Atlantic region, but throughout the world.

We view the emerging Atlantic Community as an open global region, not as an exclusive bloc. Each of our countries are enriched by our many other associations; our well-being is tied to developments around the globe. Yet the Atlantic Community can be a laboratory of trends and experiences that may facilitate greater cooperation on global issues. Our shared commitment to democracy, good governance, human rights, human dignity and a culture of lawfulness positions the Atlantic Hemisphere as a Community in which established and emerging powers can formulate shared approaches to strengthen the legitimacy and effectiveness of international rules-based governance mechanisms.

WE PLEDGE TO ADVANCE A NEW ATLANTIC COMMUNITY THAT:

- harnesses the Atlantic energy renaissance to boost traditional, unconventional and renewable energy production, facilitate energy access for millions across the Atlantic space, and build a bridge to a low-carbon future;

- opens trade and investment across the Atlantic Basin, including in ways that encourage and strengthen trade and investment in the world as a whole;

- ensures that our people share the benefits of economic growth and opportunity through improved innovation, education, training and mobility;

- makes reducing poverty and inequality a central economic goal, facilitated by inclusive economic growth; greater social mobility; and equality of opportunity.

- contributes to more effective international aid and development efforts;

- safeguards our common heritage—the Atlantic Ocean;

- promotes human security across the entire region;

- enhances cooperation based on shared beliefs in principles of democracy, respect for human rights and the rule of law, and works to advance cultures of lawfulness and effective democratic governance throughout the Atlantic Basin and beyond.

This new Atlantic Community will become a reality only if we work together actively to create it. We reaffirm our support for the continued development of the Atlantic Basin Initiative as a public-private network dedicated to producing tangible benefits for the people of our region. We commit to helping the Initiative to expand its economic, energy and security dialogues and to advance its specific work projects.

We ask the leaders of our governments to give life to this new Atlantic Community.

We ask business leaders to establish an Atlantic Business Forum to facilitate regional trade and investment and encourage the further development of business networks throughout the Hemisphere.

We ask leaders of non-governmental groups and civil society actors to forge new Atlantic networks to facilitate greater human opportunity through education and civic engagement across our entire region.

As members of the Atlantic Basin Initiative we are committed to deepening our spirit of community based on our shared vision of achieving greater human dignity, liberty, opportunity, security and prosperity for our peoples. We welcome others to our cause.

TABLE OF CONTENTS

ATLANTIC RISING

With little fanfare, the Atlantic Basin is becoming a central arena of globalization and a microcosm of key global trends, including the diffusion of power, deepening interdependencies, and spreading transnational risks. Largely unnoticed by pundits and politicians, Atlantic peoples are engaging and interacting in a whole host of ways that are shifting the contours of hemispheric interdependence and global power. The Atlantic Basin is rapidly becoming the world's energy reservoir. It is the world's most heavily traveled ocean, hosts the most global commerce, and has become the inland sea to the vast majority of the world's democratic countries. It is the warmest and most saline of the major oceans, hosts the world's richest fishing resources, and offers the most immediate opportunities for "blue growth" strategies to harvest its riches. Yet it is a region of extreme wealth and poverty. We are on the front lines of global climate change, greater superstorms and rising sea levels. Together we are threatened by a growing pan-Atlantic nexus of drugs, guns and terror.[1]

The well-being of people across our vast region is increasingly influenced by interrelated flows of people and energy, money and weapons, goods and services, technology and terror, drugs and crime. Atlantic Basin societies are benefiting from greater access to each other's markets, resources, and talent. But as growing Atlantic interdependencies spawn new opportunities, they are also generating new vulnerabilities along the interrelated arteries and nodes upon which our societies depend, requiring mutual efforts to promote human security by enhancing the resilience of these networks and the critical functions of societies across the Atlantic space.

Despite growing ties in energy, commerce, human security, norms and values, as well as issues related to the Atlantic Ocean itself, governance mechanisms and diplomatic cooperation with a pan-Atlantic frame of mind are in their infancy. A variety of cooperative mechanisms and public-private networks are slowly beginning to redraw the political map of the Atlantic. Yet on the whole there is a growing need for new approaches to governance across what may fairly be called the new Atlantic Hemisphere.

Historical legacies and political sensitivities have stunted the development of a truly "Atlantic" consciousness. Yet an Atlantic lens brings surprising new vectors into sight, and a host of developments suggests that broad, interwoven hemispheric cooperation may be possible.

KEY **RECOMMENDATIONS**

ENERGY

An Atlantic Energy Renaissance is setting the global pace for energy innovation and redrawing global maps for oil, gas, and renewables. The Atlantic Basin is now a central energy reservoir for the world and will become even more so in coming decades. Atlantic Basin countries are increasingly bound together through the production, trade, transit and consumption of energy. Yet no framework exists to allow for deepening transnational energy collaboration, which is essential for tackling pressing problems of energy access and sustainable development in the Atlantic Basin.

- Create an Atlantic Energy Forum (AEF) to:
    - facilitate and develop Atlantic Basin energy trade and investment;
    - Improve energy efficiency, energy access, environmental protection and corporate social responsibility in Atlantic energy sectors; and
    - draft an Atlantic Charter for Sustainable Energy that defines the terms of joint or coordinated Atlantic Basin action in a broad range of areas.

- Create an Atlantic Action Alliance for Renewables Deployment and the Reduction of Energy Poverty to facilitate contacts among renewables entrepreneurs, regulatory officials and policymakers, finance mechanisms and technical assistance programs.

- Develop a Cooperative Atlantic Biofuels Initiative, inspired and underpinned by the Basin's current global dominance in such energy, to advance an effective multilateral commodity regime for advanced biofuels and collaboration in the realm of biofuels research, development, investment, production, distribution and regulation, while addressing potential risks posed by large-scale public support of biofuels.

ECONOMIC GROWTH AND HUMAN DEVELOPMENT

More commerce flows within the Atlantic Basin than any other. Never have so many workers and consumers entered the Atlantic economy as quickly or as suddenly as in the past fifteen years. Growing commercial connections across the Atlantic Hemisphere offer considerable potential. But they are challenged by a range of developments, from stalled multilateral and bi-regional trade negotiations, domestic protectionist challenges, trade-distorting measures and absence of pan-Atlantic economic governance mechanisms. The Atlantic Hemisphere accounts for over half of global GDP, yet it is a region of extreme wealth and poverty. Growing inequality and lack of social mobility within countries damages social cohesion, economic efficiency, and political stability. The landscape for development cooperation has also changed. Countries that were once poor have became economic powerhouses and started their own foreign aid programs. A new aid architecture should arise: "new" donors should primarily focus on transfer of knowledge, while "traditional" donors focus on continued transfer of financial resources to poor countries that need external concessional resources. We should be guided by reforms that have catapulted fragile states to high middle income countries.

- **Promote Prosperity Through Freer Trade and Investment**
    - Bring the Doha Round of multilateral trade negotiations to a successful conclusion.
    - Adopt the long-term goal of free and open trade and investment among the four Atlantic continents.
    - Conclude current sub-regional trade and investment negotiations.
    - Ensure that the Transatlantic Trade and Investment Partnership, or TTIP, is part of an open architecture of international trade, and open to accession or association by third countries.
    - Harmonize trade preference arrangements for low-income African countries.
    - Agree on standard operating principles by state-owned enterprises.
    - Lead the global debate with regard to rules prohibiting exchange rate manipulation.

- **Reduce Poverty and Inequality**
    - Make reducing poverty and inequality a central economic goal, facilitated by inclusive economic growth; greater social mobility; and equality of opportunity, and included in the post-Millennium Development Goals 2015 development agenda.
    - Enhance social mobility by expanding and improving education and adopting less regressive public spending and sustainable social policies targeted at the poor.
    - Remove obstacles that impede equal access to opportunities.

- **Intensify Development Cooperation**
    - OECD Members should implement the commitments they made in the Paris Declaration and the Accra Agenda for Action.
    - All Atlantic Partners should implement the commitments they made in the Busan Partnership Document and participate actively in the Global Partnership for Effective Development Cooperation.

- All Atlantic Partners should join the International Aid Transparency Initiative.

- Atlantic Partners should chart a next-generation development agenda that
    > *promotes transparency and accountability regarding natural resource management;*
    > *exempts humanitarian aid from food export controls; and*
    > *advances such issues as investment and services, infrastructure, education, energy, the environment, climate change mitigation, business facilitation, and good governance.*

THE ATLANTIC OCEAN—OUR COMMON HERITAGE

Together we share a common ocean and bear joint responsibility in addressing the challenges and opportunities it presents. These include the Atlantic's role in carbon storage; more powerful storms due to the warming ocean and rising sea levels; possible changes to the Earth's thermohaline system; sustainable fisheries management; cooperative maritime governance; and the explosive growth in marine "dead zones." At the same time, Atlantic companies and countries are leading global efforts at "blue growth"—harnessing the untapped potential of the ocean to create sustainable jobs and growth, in areas such as blue energy, aquaculture, tourism, marine mineral resources and blue biotechnology.

- We call on public and private leaders to engage on common Atlantic issues; we intend to form an Atlantic Ocean Forum to advance pan-Atlantic cooperation.

HUMAN SECURITY

Drugs, human trafficking, arms flows, cyber threats, manipulation of social media, money laundering, corruption, piracy, political instability, and terrorist infiltration are all becoming concerns of pan-Atlantic scope. Left unchecked, expanding insecurity in the Atlantic Basin could undermine global trade, regional development and political stability in the region. Given the transnational nature of these growing threats, singular efforts are unlikely to prove effective. Moreover, growing flows of energy, commerce and people across the Atlantic are creating new opportunities, yet they are also creating vulnerabilities that can lead to disruption of such critical functions as transportation, energy flows, medical services, food supply chains and business systems, communications, and financial networks. These developments call for private-public partnerships and close interactions among governments, the private sector, the scientific community, and non-governmental organizations.

- **Create an Atlantic Human Security Forum** to consider concerted pan-Atlantic action against common threats, such as drugs/crime, human trafficking, piracy, terrorism and natural disasters. The member states of the Organization of American States, the African Union, and the European Union should engage with each other as well as private stakeholders to address these challenges.

- **Create a public-private Atlantic Movement Management Initiative** to align security and resilience with commercial imperatives in Atlantic movement systems, including shipping, air transport, and cyberspace.

CULTIVATE CULTURES OF LAWFULNESS AND EFFECTIVE DEMOCRATIC GOVERNANCE

With fits and starts, the Atlantic Hemisphere is coalescing around basic aims regarding democratic domestic governance. Setbacks abound and challenges remain. But a growing commitment to democratic norms and practices offers a foundation upon which established and emerging powers alike can bolster weak democracies; halt democratic backsliding; and cultivate cultures of lawfulness. The Atlantic Hemisphere also offers diverse models of democratic practice that can be relevant to broader global debates about effective and responsive governance.

- **We pledge to advance our cooperation based on a shared belief in principles of democracy, respect for human rights and the rule of law, and to work to advance these principles throughout the Atlantic region.**

- **Consideration should be given to creation of an Atlantic Peer Review Mechanism,** a voluntary arrangement by which reform leaders consult with peers who have had personal experience with reform, drawing on experience gained from the African Peer Review Mechanism of the African Union.

  - We are prepared to deploy small teams composed of our Eminent Persons, together with relevant experts, to work with reformers across the Atlantic Basin who may request such advice and counsel.

THE ATLANTIC BASIN IS RECASTING THE WORLD'S ENERGY FUTURE.

I. AN ATLANTIC ENERGY RENAISSANCE

The Atlantic Basin is recasting the world's energy future. An Atlantic Energy Renaissance is setting the global pace for energy innovation and redrawing global maps for oil, gas, and renewables as new players and technologies emerge, new conventional and unconventional sources come online, energy services boom, and opportunities appear all along the energy supply chain and across the entire Atlantic space. Together these developments are shifting the center of gravity for global energy supply from the Middle East to the Atlantic Hemisphere. Over the next 20 years the Atlantic is likely to become the energy reservoir of the world and a net exporter of many forms of energy to the Indian Ocean and Pacific Ocean Basins. Already 21 percent of China's oil imports come from the Atlantic Basin. Furthermore, nearly an identical share (around 35%) of all world oil imports now comes from the Atlantic Basin (including the Mediterranean) as from the Middle East.[2]

The Atlantic Basin currently accounts for over one-third of global oil and gas production and hosts nearly 60 percent of the presumed world total of technically recoverable shale gas reserves, 12 percent of conventional gas reserves, and 40 percent of the world's proven petroleum reserves. These shares are likely to rise in coming years, fueled by unconventional and offshore oil and gas, shale gas, new techniques for synthetic fuels production, cleaner fossil fuel technology, and traditional and modern renewable energies.[3]

The most immediate vector is North America's changing energy outlook. The United States depends considerably more on the Atlantic Basin than the Middle East for its imported energy,

even as it has reduced its overall energy dependence via surging domestic oil and gas production, driven in large part by hydraulic fracturing and horizontal drilling techniques that have unlocked previously inaccessible reserves of oil and gas. In 2012 shale gas accounted for only 2 percent in 2000, and will soon account for about half of total U.S. gas production. The United States has become a net exporter of refined petroleum products for the first time since 1949. In 2014, U.S. oil imports are projected to fall to their lowest level in a quarter century. The International Energy Agency (IEA) expects the United States to overtake Russia in 2015 as the leading producer of natural gas and to overtake Saudi Arabia in 2017 as the world's

leading producer of oil. Canada is the fifth largest energy producer in the world; energy-related products represent 6.7 percent of GDP and 23 percent of Canadian exports. It is poised to become even more of a global export force in the future as it diversifies its markets beyond its traditional U.S. partner. Mexico's oil reserves are comparable to those of Kuwait. Under President Enrique Peña Nieto it is opening its protectionist energy sector to billions in foreign investment. The Gulf of Mexico, the most developed offshore oil-and-gas region in the world, has rebounded following the 2010 Deepwater Horizon disaster and is poised for strong growth. Analysts predict that rig count will double by 2017 and Gulf of Mexico oil flows will increase by nearly 28 percent by 2022 to 1.8 million b/d.[4]

Over the next 20 years the Atlantic is likely to become the energy reservoir of the world and a net exporter of many forms of energy to the Indian Ocean and Pacific Ocean Basins.

North America's energy revival is dramatic. But energy dynamics across the Southern Atlantic are also driving change. Brazil, already endowed with rich hydropower and a world-class biofuels industry, is likely to emerge as a major oil exporter with the capacity to pump 2 million b/d from as much as 100 billion barrels of oil buried in pre-salt deepwater reserves. Brazilian exploration and discoveries off Ghana have spurred a deep offshore boom all along the Atlantic coasts of South America and Africa, from Suriname-Guyana to Argentina and from Morocco to Namibia. Venezuela has some of the largest oil and natural gas reserves in the world; its non-conventional oil deposits are estimated to roughly equal the world's reserves of conventional oil. Colombia's oil and gas sector account for 30 percent of its GDP. Argentina possibly has the third-largest shale gas resources after China and the United States. Nigeria and Angola are major energy producers. Geologists estimate that the Gulf of Guinea's oil and gas reserves, already among the richest in the world, are roughly triple current proven totals.[5]

North America's energy revival is dramatic. But energy dynamics across the Southern Atlantic are also driving change.

The gas revolution, encompassing unconventional gas, liquefied natural gas (LNG), and gas-to-liquids (GTL), is increasingly centered in the Atlantic. North America has become the world's high-growth area for LNG exports; facilities once built for LNG imports are now being fitted for export, and a score of new export facilities are developing, mainly along the Gulf of Mexico and the U.S. and Canadian Atlantic coasts. The United States could be a net LNG exporter by as early as 2016 and an overall net natural gas exporter by 2021. Just the prospect of North American LNG exports is already changing international energy markets. LNG cargoes traditionally destined for the United States have shifted to Europe, causing spot gas prices in Europe to fall. In addition, cheap coal displaced from the U.S. power sector is now being exported to Europe, further dampening gas demand and prices. These developments have forced Russia to break the gas-oil price linkage it has traditionally imposed on dependent customers and to renegotiate lower prices to Poland and Germany. Deloitte estimates that U.S. LNG exports to Europe could displace up to 22 percent of Russian gas exports to Europe and reduce considerably the price Russians receive.[6]

The Atlantic Basin is not only central to global energy supply; it is also driving global energy innovation. The Atlantic is the cradle of the modern biofuels industry and home to well over 80 percent of current global biofuels production and trade. It also accounts for more than 70 percent of global installed renewable energy capacity. A wide range of renewables—from bioenergy to solar and wind power—are rolling out in the Atlantic faster than in the Indian or Pacific Basins.[7]

> The Atlantic is the cradle of the modern biofuels industry and home to well over 80 percent of current global biofuels production and trade.

Germany's *Energiewende* is an audacious gamble to pioneer a new super-efficient, hyper-competitive industrial model. Northern European producers are world-beaters in a range of renewables and energy-saving production. The European Union has set ambitious targets to reduce its greenhouse gas emissions; raise the share of renewables in its energy consumption, and improve its energy efficiency. Major energy innovation is occurring in the North Atlantic, but Brazil is also a global leader in renewable energy

innovation. South Africa, too, has made impressive strides in synthetic transportation fuels while Morocco is a pioneer among developing countries in solar power.

> Efforts by Brazil, South Africa and Morocco to use energy to drive national development plans are being emulated by other southern Atlantic countries.

Atlantic energy dynamics are driving greater collaboration across the full Atlantic Basin and deepening and broadening Atlantic energy trade and investment. Despite the increasingly global nature of many energy markets, regional Atlantic Basin markets exist for crude oil, LNG, coal, and petroleum-derivative products.[8] Intra-Atlantic Basin trade already accounts for around 30 percent of both the global petroleum and LNG markets. Efforts by Brazil, South Africa and Morocco to use energy to drive national development plans are being emulated by other southern Atlantic countries. Brazil is supporting extensive agricultural R&D in Africa focused on both foodstuffs and commodities as well potential biofuels production and export. Brazil and the United States have also been collaborating on biofuels R&D, biofuels assistance to Latin American, Caribbean and Africa countries, and have initiated consultations aimed at designing a standardized international commodity regime for biofuels. European-North African initiatives such as Medgrid are developing ambitious energy networks.[9] New international finance mechanisms are poised to facilitate public and private investment in renewable energy and energy efficiency, and to roll out an increasingly low-carbon economy in the developing world.[10]

Such innovation could have a particularly dramatic impact in Africa, which is still characterized by deep pockets of energy poverty. Africa has the lowest electrification rate of all the world's regions—only 26 percent of households—leaving as many as 547 million people without access to electricity, nearly half of the world's energy have-nots. Meanwhile, some 75 percent of Africans still depend on traditional biomass for cooking and heating, with devastating consequences for people and the environment.[11]

An incipient Atlantic energy system is quietly taking shape that offers both capacity and potential to boost traditional energy production, facilitate access to energy for millions, build a bridge to a low carbon future, and lay the foundation for potential energy-related collaboration and governance across the Atlantic space.

The IEA estimates the cost of putting in place universal access to modern energy by 2030 at 48 billion dollars per year—only 3 percent of what experts expect to be invested in energy projects globally over the next eighteen years.[12] Expanding energy accessibility can reduce poverty and infant mortality, improve education, advance environmental sustainability, and accelerate economic growth and prosperity. A number of African development organizations are cooperating in the design, funding and construction of the Grand Inga, the world's largest proposed hydropower scheme in the Democratic Republic of Congo. Complementarities exist between the nations of Central and Southern Africa, where the potential combination of the nascent Southern African Power Pool with the enormous hydro potential of the Congo River Basin could ultimately transform the electricity supply situation for a large part of sub-Saharan Africa, a development that would greatly facilitate Africa's goal of eliminating energy poverty without significantly contributing to future accumulations of greenhouse gases.

In short, an incipient Atlantic energy system is quietly taking shape that offers both capacity and potential to boost traditional energy production, facilitate access to energy for millions, build a bridge to a low carbon future, and lay the foundation for potential energy-related collaboration and governance across the Atlantic space. Heightened Atlantic energy links, in turn, could reduce the dependence of many Atlantic Basin countries on Eurasian energy sources and take pressure off their intensifying competition with China and India over energy from some of the world's most unstable regions.[13]

The IEA estimates the cost of putting in place universal access to modern energy by 2030 at 48 billion dollars per year —only 3 percent of what experts expect to be invested in energy projects globally over the next eighteen years.

ATLANTIC ENERGY DYNAMICS ARE DRIVING GREATER COLLABORATION ACROSS THE FULL ATLANTIC BASIN AND DEEPENING AND BROADENING ATLANTIC ENERGY TRADE AND INVESTMENT.

WITH THESE PRINCIPLES AND PERSPECTIVES IN MIND, WE CALL FOR THE CREATION OF AN ATLANTIC ENERGY FORUM (AEF) TO:

FACILITATE AND DEVELOP ATLANTIC BASIN ENERGY TRADE AND INVESTMENT, TO BE ACHIEVED BY MEANS OF:

- an open and competitive market for energy products, materials, equipments and services;

- removal of technical, administrative and other barriers to trade in energy and associated equipment, technologies and energy-related services;

- collaborative efforts to elimination of illicit trade in energy;

- improved access to energy resources, and exploration and development thereof on a commercial basis;

- access on commercial terms to technologies for the exploration, development and use of energy resources;

- modernization, renewal and rationalization by industry of services and installations for the production, conversion, transport, distribution and use of energy;

- best possible access to capital, including public-private partnership financial conditions, particularly through appropriate existing financial institutions;

- further development and interconnection of energy transport infrastructure within the Atlantic Basin, and improved access to such infrastructure for international transit purposes.

IMPROVE ENERGY EFFICIENCY, ENERGY ACCESS, ENVIRONMENTAL PROTECTION AND CORPORATE SOCIAL RESPONSIBILITY IN ATLANTIC ENERGY SECTORS, IN PARTICULAR BY CONSIDERING:

- mechanisms and conditions for using energy as economically and efficiently as possible, including, as appropriate, regulatory and market-based instruments;

- mechanisms and conditions for improving energy access and eliminating energy poverty;

- the relationships between energy and development;

- possible collaborative frameworks to promote corporate social responsibility on the part of actors and agents in Atlantic Basin energy sectors;

- exchange of experience on the fiscal aspects of energy;

- promotion of energy mixes designed to minimize negative environmental consequences in cost-effective ways, including through:

    > *market-oriented energy prices reflective of environmental costs and benefits;*

    > *efficient and coordinated policy measures related to energy;*

    > *use of new and economical renewable energies and other clean technologies;*

    > *achieving and maintaining a high level of nuclear safety and ensuring effective cooperation in this field.*

CREATE AN ATLANTIC CHARTER FOR SUSTAINABLE ENERGY that defines the terms of joint or coordinated Atlantic Basin action in the following fields:

- co-ordination of Atlantic Basin energy policies—within the framework of state sovereignty and sovereign rights over energy resources—based on the principle of non-discrimination and on market-oriented price formation, taking due account of environmental concerns;

- formulation of stable and transparent legal frameworks creating conditions for the development of energy resources;

- liberalization of trade in energy, and open access to markets;

- promotion and protection of energy investments;

- dissemination of relevant best practices, safety principles and guidelines;

- promotion of energy efficiency, energy access, corporate social responsibility and environmental protection;

- mutual access to technical and economic data, consistent with proprietary rights;

- research, technological development, innovation and dissemination;

- education and training.

We further recommend the creation and promotion of an Atlantic Action Alliance for Renewables Deployment and the Reduction of Energy Poverty to supplement the content and action of the Atlantic Charter for Sustainable Energy.

This Atlantic Action Alliance would bring together energy and climate NGOs and action tanks, small and medium size enterprises, renewables manufacturers, regulatory officials and policy makers, international, regional and local financial institutions, and representatives of public-private partnerships and entities working in the realm of sustainable development. Particular attention would be placed on adaptation to and mitigation of climate change.

This cross-sector alliance would explore the potentials for synergies with the Atlantic Charter process and the Atlantic Energy Forum. The Alliance would develop a mechanism for putting actual and potential renewables entrepreneurs on the ground into contact with finance mechanisms, regulatory officials and policymakers, technical assistance programs and facilities, so as to stimulate more rapid development.

The Alliance's goals would be to offer advice for policy, locate potential niches, identify investment projects and financial resources, provide a link between small-and-medium sized enterprises and existing and evolving global support networks, and to contribute, where possible, to remove barriers to sustainable development.

EXPANDING ENERGY ACCESSIBILITY CAN REDUCE POVERTY AND INFANT MORTALITY, IMPROVE EDUCATION, ADVANCE ENVIRONMENTAL SUSTAINABILITY, AND ACCELERATE ECONOMIC GROWTH.

Third, we recommend development of a cooperative Atlantic biofuels initiative, inspired and underpinned by the Basin's current global dominance in such energy. Such a cooperative scheme in the realm of Atlantic biofuels would be helpful with regard to (1) the international effort to create an effective multilateral commodity regime for biofuels; (2) collaboration in the realm of biofuels research, development, investment, production, distribution and regulation, particularly regarding second-generation "cellulosic" biofuels technology; (3) the potential distortions of, or risks posed by, large-scale public support and/or use of biofuels, to food security, the environment, economic development and trade; and (4) rationalization and standardization of current biofuels data, which is plagued by inconsistencies. Pan-Atlantic agreements in this area would not only advance the industry across the Atlantic Basin, they could form the core of global approaches.

NEVER HAVE SO MANY WORKERS AND CONSUMERS ENTERED THE ATLANTIC ECONOMY AS QUICKLY OR AS SUDDENLY AS IN THE PAST FIFTEEN YEARS.

II. ECONOMIC GROWTH AND HUMAN DEVELOPMENT

More commerce flows within the Atlantic Basin than any other. Never have so many workers and consumers entered the Atlantic economy as quickly or as suddenly as in the past fifteen years. Despite the rise of other powers and recent economic turbulence, North America and Europe remain the fulcrum of the world economy, each other's most important and profitable market and largest source of onshored jobs. No other commercial artery is as integrated. And while rapidly developing countries in Latin America and Africa are best known for the inexpensive goods and commodities they supply to the rest of the world, their consumers are also connecting with the global marketplace, and in coming years they will become major engines of the global economy. Parts of Africa are already among the fastest growing regions of the world. According to Credit Suisse and the IMF, on several indicators Africa is better positioned than the Asian Tigers before their explosive growth in the 1980s and 1990s. North-South American commercial ties are burgeoning, and Europe's commercial ties to both Latin America and Africa are substantial. The weakest links are those between Latin America and Africa, but those connections are also the most dynamic. Moreover, today's value chains, geared to trade in tasks, hold potential for less developed southern Atlantic countries, since it is much easier to develop capabilities in a narrow range of tasks than in integrated production of an entire product.[14] When the dust clears from the economic and financial crisis, the character and nature of economic globalization may be significantly changed with respect to capital flows, production chains, and trade patterns. Think "Made in Mexico" and "Made in Ghana," not just "Made in China."

Merchandise trade among the four Atlantic Basin continents accounts for half the global total, and more than doubled over the last decade to $2.14 trillion in 2012. The NAFTA countries export more to their Atlantic partners than to the rest of the world. Americans sell three times as many merchandise exports to Europe as they do to China. New York exports 7 times, Texas 4 times, and California twice as much to Europe as to China. The EU sells the United States nearly twice the goods it sells China and nearly 7 times what it sells to India. Latin American and Caribbean countries export more than twice as much to their Atlantic partners as to the rest of the world. Latin American exports to the eurozone are 40 percent more than to China. Brazil is the single biggest exporter of agricultural products to the EU. And over half of Africa's merchandise exports go to Atlantic destinations.[15]

While rapidly developing countries in Latin America and Africa are best known for the inexpensive goods and commodities they supply to the rest of the world, their consumers are also connecting with the global marketplace, and in coming years they will become major engines of the global economy.

The Atlantic's profile is also being raised, somewhat paradoxically, by the rise of the Pacific, in at least two ways. First, trade between Atlantic and non-Atlantic markets has boomed. China in particular has become an important trading partner for all Atlantic continents, and China's trade with Africa and Latin America has grown faster than with North America and Europe. Yet the trade of both southern Atlantic continents with China resembles traditional colonial patterns. For instance, 90 percent of Brazilian exports to China consists of commodities, while 90 percent of Brazilian imports from China consists of manufactured goods. The pattern is similar throughout Africa.

South-North Atlantic trade, in contrast, is far more complementary; Brazil's merchandise trade with the United States is evenly balanced between commodities and manufactured goods. Such imbalances are provoking questions on both southern continents about the value of becoming locked into colonial-style trading relationships at a time when countries on each continent are working to diversify their respective economies.

Second, booming Atlantic-Pacific sea trade has created new port facilities throughout the Atlantic Basin, especially along its southern shores, and more are coming. In 2014 the Panama Canal is marking its 100th birthday by doubling its capacity, expanding ocean-to-ocean connections and altering global shipping patterns. Large new deepwater port facilities are being developed in Santos, Suape, and Açu in Brazil; at Lobito in Angola; and at Walvis Bay in Namibia. Spain's Algeciras and Morocco's massive Tanger-Med complex are growing in importance. And existing port cities along the Gulf of Mexico and the U.S. east coast are scrambling to revamp their infrastructure to berth megaships coming from and going to the Pacific and other Atlantic destinations.[16] Moreover, melting ice in the Arctic Ocean is opening new and shorter shipping routes from East Asia to and from Eastern North America and Europe. The U.S. government estimates that cargo transport via the Northern Sea Route alone will increase from 1.8 million tons in 2010 to 64 million tons by as soon as 2020, as ice cover declines.

When the dust clears from the economic and financial crisis, the character and nature of economic globalization may be significantly changed with respect to capital flows, production chains, and trade patterns.

Goods trade paints a partial picture of the rising Atlantic. But the truly dynamic and distinctive nature of pan-Atlantic commerce is only apparent once both investment and services are included.

It is the dynamic interaction between investment and trade that distinguishes the pan-Atlantic economy from all others. Foreign investment and affiliate sales power pan-Atlantic commerce and provide millions of jobs. Affiliate sales on either side of the Atlantic are more than double comparable sales in the entire Asia/Pacific. Much of this is driven by the foreign direct investment ties between the United States and Europe which, with combined annual sales exceeding $4 trillion, dwarf any other bilateral trade or trade/investment relationship in the world.[17] EU investment in the United States accounts for 74% of total foreign direct investment in the U.S. and is 27 times the level of EU investment in China and more than 55 times the level of EU investment in India. In fact, there is more European investment in a single U.S. state such as Indiana or Georgia than all U.S. investment in China, Japan and India combined.

Investment flows are also strong from the United States to Europe. Despite the rise of other markets, Europe continues to account for 56% of U.S. foreign direct investment worldwide. U.S. investment in Europe is nearly four times larger than U.S. investment in all of Asia and 13 times more than U.S. investment in the BRICs, and among the BRICs the leading destination for U.S. investment is Atlantic Brazil. Since the beginning of this century China has accounted for only about 1.2% of total global U.S. investment, less than tiny Belgium. U.S. investment in the Netherlands during this period was more than 14 times larger than in China. And in 2011 and 2012 U.S. companies have actually disinvested $6.5 billion from China while investing $428 billion in Europe. U.S. affiliate income from China and India together in 2011 ($13.1 billion) was less than half U.S. affiliate earnings in Ireland ($29 billion), which has emerged as the number one export platform in the world for American companies. Exports by U.S. companies based in Ireland alone were 5 times those of U.S. companies based in China in 2011.

The Atlantic Hemisphere is still characterized by both extreme wealth and poverty.

These numbers play out all across the Atlantic Basin. North American FDI in the Atlantic Hemisphere in 2012 was 7.5 higher than North American FDI in Asia.[18] The eurozone accounts for 40 percent of all foreign direct investment in Latin America, the EU is the biggest foreign investor in Brazil, and São Paulo hosts the largest concentration of German corporate investment outside Germany. EU foreign direct investment in South and Central America, totaling $973 billion in 2012, is more than EU foreign direct investment in all of Asia; EU foreign direct investment in the four continents of the Atlantic Hemisphere was 4 times EU foreign direct investment in Asia. Even Asian companies invest more in the Atlantic Hemisphere than in the Asian Hemisphere.[19]

The Atlantic's profile is also being raised by the rise of the Pacific.

In fact, foreign direct investment, not trade, has become the main means for North Atlantic companies to get access to high-growth emerging markets. Between 2000 and 2011, U.S. FDI stock in Latin America and the Caribbean rose 212 percent from $267 billion to $831 billion. Investment from Europe rose 185 percent between 2000 and 2010 (latest available), from €248 billion to €707 billion. Since 2000, U.S. and European firms have each invested significantly more capital in Brazil than in China. South Atlantic multinationals are increasingly following suit, preferring to invest in major developed economies, primarily in the North Atlantic, although Brazilian firms are investing billions in Africa's resource-related industries. Unlike resource-hungry China, resource-rich Brazil is investing in Africa to diversify its export markets and internationalize the production of its big companies.[20]

Services are the sleeping giant of the pan-Atlantic economy. The Atlantic is home to the world's major services economies, and Atlantic economies are each other's most important services markets.[21] Global trade in services is still less important than trade in goods, since many service activities require a local presence and many countries impose restrictions on services trade. Nonetheless, services trade has intensified and is set to expand rapidly, and Atlantic economies are poised to be major beneficiaries and drivers of the growth in global services.[22]

The United States is the largest single country trader in services, while the EU is the largest trader in services among all world regions. Most American and European jobs are in the services economy, which accounts for over 70 percent of U.S. and EU GDP. Over half of U.S. and EU services exports go to Atlantic Basin countries,[23] and each is seeing an increasing share of its services trade conducted with Latin America and Africa. Moreover, the delivery of services by foreign affiliates—driven by pan-Atlantic investments—has exploded over the past decade and is far more significant than services trade. The U.S. and EU each owe a good part of their competitive position in services globally to deep Atlantic connections in services industries provided by mutual investment flows. A good share of U.S. services exports to the world are generated by U.S. affiliates of European multinationals, just as a good share of EU services exports to the world are generated by European affiliates of U.S. multinationals.[24]

U.S. AND EUROPEAN FIRMS HAVE EACH INVESTED SIGNIFICANTLY MORE CAPITAL IN BRAZIL THAN IN CHINA.

Services are not just a North Atlantic story. Services are far more important to Atlantic economies such as Brazil, South Africa, Mexico and Colombia than to non-Atlantic economies such as Russia, India or China. Brazil's expanding services industry contributes about two-thirds of its total GDP and employs about 70 percent of its labor force. Services account for more than 50 percent of GDP in Africa's 36 non-resource-rich economies and for more than 40 percent of GDP—more than industry's share—in the continent's resource-rich economies. As income per capita in Latin America and Africa grows, and as governments seek to diversify their economies away from commodity production, demand will grow for such services as health care, education, entertainment, insurance, telecommunications and finance. Moreover, services is a growing area of commercial activity among Southern Atlantic countries, particularly in energy-related services; engineering and construction services; and education and managerial services.[25]

North Atlantic countries have offered preferential arrangements for poorer countries, for instance via the U.S. African Growth and Opportunity Act, or AGOA, and the EU's "Everything But Arms" initiative. But conflicting rules of origin and other diverse criteria render such efforts less effective than they could be, given greater coordination.

Regional agreements opening trade are far more advanced in the Atlantic Hemisphere than in the Asian Hemisphere. The EU's Single Market among 28 countries and 500 million people, NAFTA arrangements among 400 million people, the

Central American Integration System called SICA and South America's MERCOSUR have all facilitated expanded trade among regional neighbors. These are complemented by a number of bilateral free trade agreements, such as those between Chile and the MERCOSUR countries, between the U.S. and Morocco, Chile, Colombia, Peru and Panama, and between the EU and Central America. The EU-Mexico free trade agreement has boosted bilateral trade by 25 percent. The EU and Canada are finalizing a comprehensive trade and investment agreement that could do the same.

Melting ice in the Arctic Ocean is opening new and shorter shipping routes from East Asia to and from Eastern North America and Europe.

Most importantly, the EU and the United States are negotiating a Transatlantic Trade and Investment Agreement that, if successful, would not only open trade and investment across the North Atlantic but set global benchmarks on a range of norms, standards and regulatory issues. The European think tank ECIPE estimates that the free trade element alone—not the most dynamic element of a potential agreement—would boost exports about five times more than the recent U.S.-Korea free trade agreement.

Looking ahead, the Atlantic Basin is also likely to benefit from a host of additional factors—information technology advances, infrastructure improvements, new energy dynamics, better business environments, financial uncertainties, the rise of tailored services, advances in digitization, and changes in advanced and additive manufacturing—that are redrawing the world's commercial map, connecting Latin America and Africa more with global supply chains, and leading a growing number of North Atlantic companies to either re-shore or near-shore their supply chains back to the Atlantic Hemisphere. Moreover, Atlantic companies and countries are leading global efforts at "blue growth"—harnessing the untapped potential of the ocean to create sustainable jobs and growth, in areas such as blue energy, aquaculture, tourism, marine mineral resources and blue biotechnology.[26]

The Atlantic is home to the world's major services economies, and Atlantic economies are each other's most important services markets.

The Atlantic partners could also assume a pioneering role in a number of other areas. They could lead by ending trade-distorting agricultural subsidies and exempting humanitarian aid from food export controls, as recommended by the Group of 20. Such initiatives seem more realistic now than in the past because of the changing outlook for agriculture from chronic surpluses to increased demand. They could lead the global debate with regard to prohibiting exchange rates manipulation to gain unfair trade advantage. The Atlantic partners could also form the core of an international services agreement that offers reciprocal liberalization to all economies willing

to join, with flexibilities for low-income countries. For Southern Atlantic countries seeking to diversify their economies, the services trade is increasingly important to boosting productivity and to lower costs of critical infrastructure development.

In short, growing commercial connections across the Atlantic Hemisphere offer considerable potential. But they are challenged by a range of developments, from stalled multilateral and bi-regional trade negotiations, domestic protectionist challenges, trade-distorting measures and absence of pan-Atlantic economic governance mechanisms. The Atlantic Hemisphere is still characterized by both extreme wealth and poverty. South Atlantic countries, many of which continue to struggle to diversify their economies, are concerned that new plurilateral initiatives could divert trade to their detriment.

WITH THESE CONSIDERATIONS IN MIND, WE CALL FOR A PAN-ATLANTIC AGENDA FOR ECONOMIC GROWTH AND HUMAN DEVELOPMENT, COMPRISED OF THE FOLLOWING ELEMENTS.

PROMOTE PROSPERITY THROUGH FREER TRADE AND INVESTMENT

We oppose strongly the creation of inward-looking trading blocs that would divert from the pursuit of global free trade. We are determined to pursue free and open trade and investment in the Atlantic in a manner that will encourage and strengthen trade and investment liberalization in the world as a whole.

SERVICES ARE THE SLEEPING GIANT OF THE PAN-ATLANTIC ECONOMY.

- **Bring the Doha Round of multilateral trade negotiations to a successful conclusion.**
The open multilateral trading system is the foundation of our economic growth. The Atlantic Community should lead the way in removing roadblocks and taking concrete steps to produce the strongest possible outcome in Geneva. Increased participation by Atlantic economies, including via an Atlantic caucus, in a strengthened WTO system will also facilitate greater cooperation across the Atlantic space.

- **Adopt the long-term goal of free and open trade and investment among the four Atlantic continents.**

  > *Create an Atlantic Business Advisory Forum to recommend concrete steps to further reduce barriers to trade and investment and to promote the free flow of goods, services and capital among our economies.*

  > *Draft an Atlantic Investment Compact based on common principles to facilitate enhanced investment as an engine for growth throughout the Atlantic space.*

- **Conclude current sub-regional trade and investment negotiations.** We welcome the Comprehensive Economic and Trade Agreement (CETA) between the EU and Canada and U.S.-EU negotiations for a Transatlantic Trade and Investment Partnership, or TTIP. We call on the EU and Mercosur to conclude their long-standing negotiations, and on leaders in the Americas to revive the goal of a "Free Trade Area of the Americas" (FTAA), in which barriers to trade and investment will be progressively eliminated. The Atlantic Business Forum should recommend how existing sub-regional and bilateral arrangements could be codified and aligned to enhance overall Atlantic and global economic cooperation.

- **Ensure that the Transatlantic Trade and Investment Partnership, or TTIP, is part of an open architecture of international trade, and open to accession or association by third countries.** TTIP promises a boost to North Atlantic economies. But unless properly designed as part of an "open architecture," the partnership could hurt the trade prospects of other countries. We urge President Obama and EU leaders to declare publicly that TTIP is indeed part of the open architecture of international trade, and to outline future modalities for accession, association, or complementary economic agreements with other countries. The United States and the European Union have common interest in demonstrating that TTIP is about trade creation, not trade diversion.

- **Harmonize trade preference arrangements for low-income African countries.** North American countries and the EU should harmonize their current hodgepodge of trade preference mechanisms for low-income African countries. Latin America could conceivably join in offering the same market access, building on preferences already given by some countries in Latin America, and on interests they have expressed within the WTO to improve market access for poorer developing countries. Such efforts should harmonize country and product coverage as well as rules of origin of current preferential arrangements, taking the best and most effective provisions of each respective program, making them compatible and updating the rules to the current trading environment.[27]

- **Agree on standard operating principles by state-owned enterprises.** The increased importance of such enterprises—in financial services, telecommunications, steel, chemicals and energy, and other natural resources— requires new rules so that private businesses can compete fairly with state capitalism. The rules need not push privatization or roll back state enterprises, but they should require transparency, commercial behavior, declarations of subsidies, nondiscrimination and open procurement.

- **Promote strategic discussions regarding infrastructure construction** to facilitate movement of goods, services and people, including forms of financing to encourage private sector investment that can create jobs and spur economic growth.

- **Lead the global debate with regard to rules prohibiting exchange rate manipulation** to gain unfair trade advantage. Brazil has already raised this issue; its Atlantic partners should support such an initiative.

REDUCE POVERTY AND INEQUALITY

Growing inequality within countries is a pressing problem for the Atlantic world, damaging social cohesion, economic efficiency, and political stability. Poverty, lack of social mobility and attempts by public officials to exclude certain groups or individuals from the economic benefits of inclusive growth can contribute to inequality. Inequality, in turn, not only implies a slower rate of poverty reduction; it further reduces social mobility, contributes to financial crises, weakens demand and prolongs recessions. Accumulated economic and social research shows conclusively that equality is an important ingredient in promoting and sustaining growth. Extreme inequality also breeds mistrust, which damages the social fabric on which democracy rests.

- We call on leaders to make reducing poverty and inequality a central economic goal, facilitated by inclusive economic growth; greater social mobility; and equality of opportunity, and included in the post-Millennium Development Goals 2015 development agenda.

- In order to enhance social mobility, we call for more efficient markets and government services; expansion and improvement of education; less regressive public spending; and for sustainable social policies targeted at the poor.

INTENSIFY DEVELOPMENT COOPERATION

Since the turn of the millennium the international landscape for development aid has changed. Countries that were once poor have became economic powerhouses and started their own foreign aid programs. Traditional donors in the OECD's Development Assistance Committee (DAC) have committed to change their programs based on lessons learned from accumulated

IT IS THE DYNAMIC INTERACTION BETWEEN INVESTMENT AND TRADE THAT DISTINGUISHES THE PAN-ATLANTIC ECONOMY FROM ALL OTHERS.

evaluations of aid effectiveness. Unfortunately, implementation has lagged and the international aid architecture has not been updated.

For aid to be effective, the most critical issue is that donors and recipients have a common understanding that donors do not develop countries. Developing countries develop themselves. Such an understanding leads to developing country ownership of the assistance program without which no aid yields lasting results. Today, less than half of technical cooperation flows are consistent with national development strategies. Aid should be integrated in the recipient's regular planning and budget systems, and where possible, donors must support developing countries with predictable multi-year funding for their home-grown programs and transfer the management of aid to the partner government.

New donors like Brazil fully understand and respect the importance of ownership; and sharing their own development experiences with emphasis on the "how-to" aspects of implementing development projects and programs creates a clear comparative advantage. Thus, a new aid architecture should arise: "new" donors should primarily focus on transfer of knowledge, while "traditional" donors focus on continued transfer of financial resources to poor countries that need external concessional resources.

Improvements in aid effectiveness and a new aid architecture would complement our proposal to harmonize trade preferences.

WE RECOMMEND THAT:

- **OECD members implement the commitments they made in the Paris Declaration and the Accra Agenda for Action;**

- **All Atlantic partners implement the commitments they made in the Busan Partnership Document and participate actively in the Global Partnership for Effective Development Cooperation;**

- **All Atlantic partners join the International Aid Transparency Initiative.**

- **Atlantic partners chart a next-generation agenda.** Atlantic partners have a shared interest in developing codes of conduct to promote transparency and accountability regarding natural resource management; exempting humanitarian aid from food export controls, as recommended by the Group of 20; and taking the lead in such next-generation development issues as investment and services, infrastructure, education, energy, the environment, efforts to adapt to and mitigate climate change, business facilitation, and good governance.[28] The Extractive Industries Transparency Initiative is one example of how such efforts could develop, with Atlantic nations taking the lead.

THE ATLANTIC OCEAN COVERS ONE-FIFTH OF THE EARTH'S SURFACE AND RECEIVES WATER FROM ABOUT HALF THE WORLD'S LAND AREA.

III. OUR COMMON HERITAGE—
THE ATLANTIC OCEAN

The Atlantic Ocean, the elongated S-shaped body of water connecting the peoples of North and South America, Europe and Africa, covers one-fifth of the earth's surface and receives water from about half the world's land area—about four times that of either the Pacific or Indian oceans. Its tributary waters begin in Glacier National Park, in the U.S. state of Montana; in the turf swamps of the Valdai Hills in central Russia; in a trickle of glacial water flowing off the Apacheta cliff in the Peruvian Andes; and in a savanna plateau just south of Lake Tanganyika in east-central Africa's Great Rift Valley. It joins the Arctic Ocean via the Greenland Sea and Smith Sound; merges with the Southern Ocean in the Antarctic Circumpolar Current; connects to the Pacific through the Drake Passage, the Straits of Magellan and the Panama Canal; and unites with the Indian Ocean at the Suez Canal and off of Cape Agulhas at Africa's southernmost tip. Although it is the world's second-largest ocean, it is far more compact than the Pacific. The shortest Atlantic crossing, between Senegal and northeastern Brazil, is 1,600 miles—about the same as between Chicago and San Francisco and less than between Tokyo and Guangzhou.[29]

The Atlantic Ocean is our common heritage. Our ocean shares problems with other oceans—pollution, degradation of marine and coastal ecosystems and marine biodiversity, and the looming effects of climate change. There are issues distinct to the Atlantic, however, that increasingly require pan-Atlantic attention.

The Atlantic serves a unique function as the locus of the planet's thermohaline system, a global circulation pattern of currents that distributes water and heat from the Equator to the poles, reducing extremes in the planet's climate. Any change to this pattern could have untold effects all across the globe, and there are indications that change is underway. Thermohaline circulation is driven by the sinking of cold, salty water at high latitudes. Yet scientists have found that North Atlantic surface waters are becoming warmer and "fresher," i.e. less salty, and thus less dense, possibly altering the trajectory and force of the Gulf Stream, the North Atlantic Current, and overall global thermohaline

circulation, with serious impacts on marine ecosystems, fishing grounds, coastal water quality and nutrient cycling, sea levels and surface climate. Some climate models project weakening of the Atlantic turnover process of up to 25 per cent by the end of this century. While the decreased influx of ocean heat could be compensated by future global warming caused by the insulating effect of carbon dioxide in the atmosphere, these two processes are unlikely to be equivalent or synchronous, and thus likely to have major disruptive effects on human activity, not just along coasts but across continents.[30]

Warmer oceans and rising sea levels interact to enhance the destructive potential of more powerful storms. Their impact may be greatest at particular hot spot areas experiencing greater than average sea level rise—such as the U.S. East Coast.

Second, the Atlantic plays a particularly important role in carbon storage. The oceans are the greatest carbon reservoirs, containing far more carbon than either the atmosphere or the terrestrial biosphere, and absorbing about a quarter of the carbon dioxide humans release into the atmosphere every year. While this process takes place everywhere across the ocean surface, cold salty water in the North Atlantic and in an ocean belt between 30 and 50 degrees south latitude absorb enormous amounts of gases before it sinks, and then transports them to much greater ocean depths, primarily at four polar convection points, three of which are

in the Atlantic. Unfortunately, the oceans are not absorbing carbon dioxide as fast as humans are emitting it, and the high levels that are being absorbed by the Atlantic are raising acidity levels, with potentially cascading effects throughout the marine food chain and the overall structure of marine ecosystems.

Third, warmer oceans and rising sea levels interact to enhance the destructive potential of more powerful storms. Their impact may be greatest at particular hot spot areas experiencing greater than average sea level rise—such as the U.S. East Coast. Sea levels on the heavily populated stretch of coast from Cape Hatteras to Boston have accelerated roughly three to four times the global average.[31] Researchers have extrapolated that sea levels at New York City could rise by up to 11.4 inches by 2100—in addition to the roughly 3 feet of average sea level rise expected worldwide by then.[32] Superstorm Sandy was fueled by much-higher-than-average sea-surface temperatures, but higher sea levels heightened its destructive impact. As coastal regions all along the Atlantic struggle to cope with future calamities, extremely expensive surge barrier projects such as those around London, Rotterdam and Venice are likely to remain exceptions. Just as important could be new mechanisms of pan-Atlantic exchange of best practice regarding integrated coastal risk management.

North Atlantic surface waters are becoming warmer and "fresher," possibly altering the trajectory and force of the Gulf Stream, the North Atlantic Current, and overall global thermohaline circulation,

Fourth, concern about the explosive growth in the size and number of marine "dead zones," areas where the deep water is so low in dissolved oxygen that sea creatures can't survive. Marine dead zones have grown ten-fold globally in the past 50 years and almost thirty-fold in the United States since 1960. All told, there are over 400 dead zones worldwide. Most are in the Atlantic. Many occur naturally, but human-induced changes, such as agricultural runoff, have expanded such zones and changed their nature. The New Jersey-size dead zone at the Mississippi's outlet into the Gulf of Mexico has received considerable attention. But a massive low oxygen zone off of West Africa is growing, encroaching upon habitats of tuna, billfish and other species, forcing them into already overfished areas.[33] This is a further phenomenon appropriate for pan-Atlantic concern.

The Atlantic plays a particularly important role in carbon storage.

Four of the Atlantic's seven marine fishing areas lead the world with 50 percent or more of stocks overfished, and in the other three areas up to 30 percent of fish stocks are overexploited, due in large part to unsustainable fishery subsidies. As traditional fishing grounds becoming less fruitful,

fisheries move to new areas and stocks as catches diminish.[34] In addition, the Northeast Atlantic offers the clearest evidence to date that rising water temperatures are shifting the ranges and variations of warmer water marine organisms towards the poles. These changing patterns are creating new challenges for sustainable fisheries management and affecting fisheries catch probabilities, potentially benefiting the Arctic, and Atlantic temperate waters, at the expense of the Gulf of Mexico and Atlantic equatorial waters.

Warmer oceans and rising sea levels interact to enhance the destructive potential of more powerful storms. Their impact may be greatest at particular hot spot areas experiencing greater than average sea level rise—such as the U.S. East Coast.

In addition, as global fishing fleets increasingly focus their efforts on the southern Atlantic as traditional stocks diminish, control of illegal, unregulated, and unreported fishing presents a growing challenge.[35] There is a vacuum in terms both of national maritime governance structures in most littoral states and any overarching system of cooperative governance. Those regional fisheries commissions that exist have not proven particularly effective, nor do they cooperate very well.

Despite this multitude of issues, Atlantic Ocean governance is patchy. Some North Atlantic mechanisms are at work, but South Atlantic arrangements are uneven and weak, and no overarching pan-Atlantic framework exists.[36] In the case of pollution from ships, for instance, the so-called Bonn Agreement provides for cooperative arrangements with regard to such eventualities in the northeastern Atlantic, but equivalent arrangements do not exist for other quadrants of the Atlantic. Broad cooperative mechanisms such as the European Maritime Safety Agency (EMSA) do not exist in the southern Atlantic beyond national organizations.[37]

All told, there are over 400 dead zones worldwide. Most are in the Atlantic.

Northern Atlantic partners could consider offering satellite photos along major maritime routes to Southern Atlantic partners willing to receive them. Consideration could also be given to an Atlantic Coast Guard Forum to facilitate operational cooperation and exchange of best practices, including among magistrates of coastal states with regard to investigation methods. A study group sponsored by the German Marshall Fund of the United States has recommended the creation of a Southern Atlantic forum within which countries can share their own ideas on ocean governance and maritime policy and profit from the experience of the North. Over time, the activities of this forum could lead southern states to set up governance mechanisms for sustainable and safe shared development.[38] We endorse these recommendations, perhaps buttressed by annual engagement at the full pan-Atlantic level.

A related pan-Atlantic development is the so-called "blue growth" agenda, which encompasses various initiatives to harness the untapped potential of oceans, seas and coasts for jobs and growth.[39] Various aspects merit attention. The first is blue energy, or energy derived from the ocean. Offshore and deep-sea exploration and extraction of traditional fossil fuels is advancing off all Atlantic coasts, yet there are no international safety standards for offshore energy installations other than those defined by individual companies. Opportunities for private-public partnerships could be on offer related to other ocean energy technologies, such as offshore wind, wave and tidal devices, and ocean thermal energy conversion. The exploitation and mining of minerals from the sea is also advancing and could extend into deeper water. Global annual turnover of marine mineral mining is expected to grow from virtually nothing to €5 billion in the next 10 years and up to €10 billion by 2030, and yet the Law of the Sea and related conventions do not fully address such developments, amidst rising environmental concerns. Finally, blue biotechnology, which could result in ground-breaking drugs developed from marine organisms, also poses challenges of standards and governance. In each of these areas appropriate governance mechanisms are lacking. Atlantic nations could lead.

WE CALL ON PUBLIC AND PRIVATE LEADERS TO ENGAGE ON COMMON ATLANTIC ISSUES; WE INTEND TO FORM AN ATLANTIC OCEAN FORUM TO ADVANCE PAN-ATLANTIC COOPERATION.

THE OCEANS ARE NOT ABSORBING CARBON DIOXIDE AS FAST AS HUMANS ARE EMITTING IT, AND THE HIGH LEVELS THAT ARE BEING ABSORBED BY THE ATLANTIC ARE RAISING ACIDITY LEVELS.

WHILE CHALLENGES OF STATE-TO-STATE SECURITY ARE GREATEST IN THE PACIFIC, CHALLENGES TO HUMAN SECURITY ARE MOST RELEVANT FOR THE ATLANTIC.

IV. HUMAN SECURITY

The international strategic community, focused largely on traditional inter-state disputes, particularly those with potentially global impact, has turned its gaze from the Atlantic because it lacks the defining conflicts, cleavages and existential flashpoints evident in the Asia-Pacific region and the Indian Ocean. As Ian Lesser has pointed out, there is no wider Atlantic equivalent to the risk of nuclear war on the Korean peninsula, the India-Pakistan conflict or the looming U.S.-Chinese strategic competition.[40] This distinction is important, but perhaps in a different way than traditionally interpreted. While challenges of state-to-state security are greatest in the Pacific, challenges to human security are most relevant for the Atlantic.

Some "traditional" conflicts certainly continue, but they tend to be small in comparison to Pacific challenges. The reopening of territorial claims in the South Atlantic, spurred in part by the discovery of new commercially profitable resources, could fuel additional tensions among Atlantic states. But larger—and common—Atlantic challenges are largely intra-state in nature. Trafficking in people, arms, drugs and money, piracy, political instability, and terrorist infiltration are all becoming concerns of pan-Atlantic scope. Human security—protecting people from violence or disruption—is likely to be more of a driver than state security when it comes to Atlantic cooperation. Furthermore, these security challenges tend to be common, and thus present an opportunity to unite efforts and test new modes of governance.

The drug trade is the most lucrative branch of organized crime, cocaine is the most profitable drug within the drug trade, and cocaine is very much an Atlantic scourge. Almost all the world's cocaine is produced in Colombia, Peru and Bolivia. The U.S. is the biggest consumer and Europe is the most lucrative market. The routes to these markets crisscross Central America as a corridor and operational base for North America and a launching pad for shipments via the Azores to Europe. They also flow from Venezuela, which accounts for half of the cocaine being supplied to Europe, via Cape Verde, Madeira and the Canary Islands; and they traverse Brazil and other parts of South America to West Africa as a logistics base and transshipment point to Europe and beyond. These drugs operations are now spreading to East, Central and South Africa as well. In addition, the conventional wisdom that the North consumes drugs and the South produces them has dissolved; consumption is growing throughout the South Atlantic—Brazil

is now the world's second largest cocaine consumer—and trafficking is growing across the North Atlantic.[41]

Additional security issues arise from the growing flows of energy, commerce and people across the Atlantic.

Other drugs, such as heroin, are also becoming pan-Atlantic challenges. Moreover, health challenges associated with drug use require holistic approaches to human security; rising addiction rates in many Latin America and Africa countries are taxing already burdened, underfunded health care systems. Across the Basin, high levels of violence and corruption associated with drug trafficking are leading authorities to go beyond criminal justice approaches and to focus more on social and health issues related to drug use, preventive measures and even legal regulation of specific drugs.[42]

The drug trade is the most lucrative branch of organized crime, cocaine is the most profitable drug within the drug trade, and cocaine is very much an Atlantic scourge.

The intersection of crime and conflict is not a new phenomenon, but globalization and communications technology have provided insurgent and terror networks with the capacity to expand their operations and connections far beyond the boundaries of their original conflict zones. For years small arms and light weapons flowed illicitly across the Atlantic from Africa to South America and up to the FARC or other insurgent groups. Now flows of drugs, arms and cash flow across the full Atlantic space.

Moreover, not only have crime cartels intruded on states; governments such as Guinea-Bissau have themselves become organized criminal enterprises bent on facilitating illicit pan-Atlantic flows. As a consequence, west Africa is in danger of becoming a black hole of intermingled trafficking, terrorism and corruption.

Atlantic Basin countries are also bound by the consequences of other human security challenges, including illegal exploitation and illicit trade of natural resources; corporate bribery; illicit diversion of assistance expenditures; the channelling of illicit flows to secrecy jurisdictions; tax evasion; cybercrime; oil bunkering (illegal tapping of pipelines); exploitation of labor; and manipulation of export (or import) prices in order to reduce the in-country tax burden and maximize externalized income, usually through a secrecy jurisdiction and a process often known as 'mispricing.' Between 2001-2010 illicit flows from Latin America were estimated at $877 billion, from Africa $357 billion.[43]

These networks of crime, corruption and terror have become the modern HIV virus of the Atlantic world.[44] Their potency is enhanced by rippling traffic in goods, services, people, drugs, money and arms that is lashing the four Atlantic continents tighter together.

TRAFFICKING IN PEOPLE, ARMS, DRUGS AND MONEY, PIRACY, POLITICAL INSTABILITY, AND TERRORIST INFILTRATION ARE ALL BECOMING CONCERNS OF PAN-ATLANTIC SCOPE.

The conventional wisdom that the North consumes drugs and the South produces them has dissolved; consumption is growing throughout the South Atlantic.

The evolving situation in Mali is emblematic. The French-led intervention was characterized as an effort to roust al-Qaeda in the Islamic Maghreb from territory twice the size of France that it had wrested from Malian authorities. But what gave the movement real potency was not the attraction of its radical ideology but its close and lucrative links to crime cartels trafficking in drugs and guns, primarily from the Americas and Europe. Latin American gun runners and narco-cartels have leapfrogged the Atlantic, using weakly governed spaces in west Africa as logistics hubs and transshipment points for destinations in Europe and beyond.[45]

This nexus of crime, drugs, guns and terror has become a pan-Atlantic challenge and requires pan-Atlantic answers.

Additional security issues arise from the growing flows of energy, commerce and people across the Atlantic. As the new Atlantic economy grows ever more connected, complex flows of capital, goods, information and people are creating new interlinked networks. Yet this dynamism also creates vulnerabilities that can lead to disruption of such critical functions as transportation, energy flows, medical services, food supply chains and business systems, communications, cyber links and financial networks. Governments are accustomed to protect their territories; now they must protect their society's critical

functions, the networks that sustain them, and the connections those networks bring with other societies. These developments call for private-public partnerships and close interactions among governments, the private sector, the scientific community, and non-governmental organizations.

A further development makes discussion of pan-Atlantic security cooperation more relevant. U.S. primacy on the high seas has guaranteed commercial maritime stability for decades, and has, therefore, been taken for granted, even as globalization has depended on it. Yet given a reduction in U.S. military spending and a renewed U.S. naval focus on the Pacific, we may be entering a phase of history in which several nations might share dominance of the high seas, rather than one as in the recent past. This situation is likely to emerge in the Atlantic before it would in the Pacific, and thus the Atlantic may become a test bed for a maritime concert of democracies dedicated to ensuring Atlantic Ocean security.[46]

The intersection of crime and conflict is not a new phenomenon, but globalization and communications technology have provided insurgent and terror networks with the capacity to expand their operations and connections far beyond the boundaries of their original conflict zones.

Taken together, these challenges present opportunity to Atlantic stakeholders to form pan-Atlantic networks oriented to ensure security of pan-Atlantic flows.

Governments are accustomed to protect their territories; now they must protect their society's critical functions, the networks that sustain them, and the connections those networks bring with other societies.

Given Southern sensitivities and discrepancies between northern and southern Atlantic governance mechanisms, these networks might usefully begin in the South. Northern Atlantic countries can provide experience and funding without a heavy footprint, and southern Atlantic countries can take on greater responsibilities for the common good of the neighborhood. Over time, new forms of cooperation on common human security challenges could increase opportunities for discussion, partnership and confidence-building among developing and developed countries in the Atlantic Hemisphere.

Such efforts would not be starting from scratch. The Praia Action Plan Against Drugs and Organized Crime, adopted by ECOWAS, is comprehensive, yet implementation has lagged. Spain, Portugal and ten South Atlantic states convened an effort in Lanzarote in 2009 to jumpstart a soft security framework focused on organized crime, illegal migration, weather monitoring, and the safeguarding of biodiversity, yet little has been done. Both initiatives could be refined and expanded to include other Atlantic partners. West and Central African countries are working on a framework for regional law enforcement operations; the Commission on the Impact of Drug-Trafficking on Governance, Security and Development in West Africa, chaired by former Nigerian President Olusegun

Obasanjo, shows promise. The Kimberley Process, which involves supply-chain policing of conflict diamonds to target weak links in ways that can enhance international effectiveness, could be a model for policing other criminal supply chains. The Extractive Industries Transparency Initiative is one of the most advanced examples of the current trend to increased transparency in government and corporate relations. Gaining greater African adherence to the Financial Action Task Force would also be useful.

Patchwork cooperation belies a diversity of views and priorities with regard to organized crime and illicit activities that has not yet been addressed adequately.

Other initiatives, such as the Mexican-led Chapultepec Consensus against transnational organized crime; the 2003 Caribbean Regional Maritime Agreement and the 2008 Caribbean Community (CARICOM) Maritime and Airspace Security Cooperation Agreement; INTERPOL's OASIS program in Africa and its cooperation with Mercosur; or cooperation programs sponsored by UNODC (the West Africa Coast Initiative or the Container Control Program), the EU (SEACOP; AIRCOP; Cocaine Route Program; COPOLAD) or the U.S. (West Africa Cooperative Security Initiative; International Law Enforcement Academies) might serve as useful orientation points for broader pan-Atlantic cooperation, as would lessons learned from the Mali intervention.

NETWORKS OF CRIME, CORRUPTION AND TERROR HAVE BECOME THE MODERN HIV VIRUS OF THE ATLANTIC WORLD.

As Atlantic commercial connections intensify, so should cooperation in countering organized crime.

Nonetheless, on the whole such efforts remain limited or uneven, often without clear prioritization and minimal national ownership. They have yet to inspire a broader pan-Atlantic architecture. In addition, patchwork cooperation belies a diversity of views and priorities with regard to organized crime and illicit activities that has not yet been addressed adequately. Related questions of governance and development must be included. A common debate and assessment of vulnerabilities across the Atlantic Basin, including specific "flow security" challenges among Atlantic Basin states, could add value. Cooperation should also be extended where similar challenges offer opportunities to learn from each other's experience. For example, lessons learned from Central America with regard to particular difficulties of fragile states serving as transit zones for drugs could be very beneficial to some West African countries.[47] And as Atlantic commercial connections intensify, so should cooperation in countering organized crime.

WITH THESE CONSIDERATIONS IN MIND, WE RECOMMEND THE FOLLOWING MEASURES:

- **Create an Atlantic Human Security Forum to consider concerted pan-Atlantic efforts to promote human security across the entire region.** Such efforts can build on a variety of sub-regional mechanisms already in place. Further steps might include, inter alia, improvement in mutual intelligence, assistance, surveillance, and interdiction capacities to combat illicit maritime activities and trafficking in drugs, arms or human beings, and strengthened networks of mutual assistance agreements among Atlantic states. Such networks could be informed by a few basic principles: agreement on military restraint; commitment to keeping sea lanes and sea lines of communication open; regular consultations on security challenges; and appropriate action against common threats such as trafficking, transnational organized crime, piracy, terrorism and natural disasters.

- **Consider the creation of a public-private Atlantic Movement Management Initiative,** the task of which would be to align security and resilience with commercial imperatives in Atlantic movement systems, including shipping, air transport, and cyberspace. Such an effort could improve cooperation among public and private stakeholders and serve potentially as a precursor for a more ambitious global governance framework.[48]

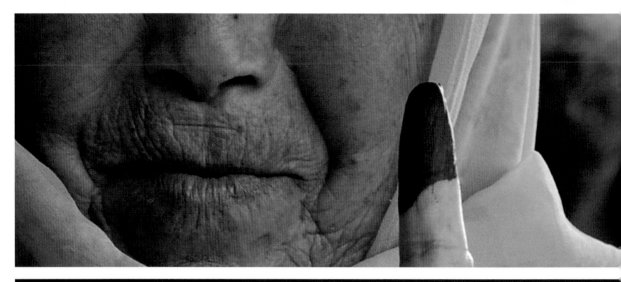

DEMOCRATIC DISENCHANTMENT, REPUDIATION OF POLITICS AND POLITICIANS, POPULIST FASHIONS, AND EXTREME SOCIETAL VIOLENCE AFFECT COUNTRIES ACROSS THE ATLANTIC SPACE.

V. CULTIVATING CULTURES OF LAWFULNESS AND EFFECTIVE DEMOCRATIC GOVERNANCE

There is yet another reason why the Atlantic offers potential as a test bed for how established and emerging powers can probe new governance approaches. The Asian Hemisphere is the hemisphere of contested norms and principles among and between open and closed societies. The Atlantic Hemisphere, in contrast, is— admittedly with fits and starts—coalescing around basic aspirations regarding domestic governance. Across the Atlantic space there is growing commitment to promote liberty, improve the efficiency of markets, and to respect human dignity. All countries in North America, the European Union and Latin America—with the exception of Cuba—are now rated partly free or better by Freedom House.[49] Africa, too, has experienced greater democracy. In 1990 Freedom House recorded just 3 African countries with multiparty political systems, universal suffrage, regular fraud-free elections and secret ballots. Today close to 60 percent of African countries are now rated partly free or better by Freedom House.

Of course, across the full Atlantic space achievement does not always match aspiration. Setbacks abound and challenges remain. Democratic disenchantment, repudiation of politics and politicians, populist fashions, and extreme societal violence affect countries across the Atlantic space.

A growing commitment to democratic norms and practices, however, offers a foundation upon which established and emerging powers alike can bolster weak democracies susceptible to organized crime cartels or terror networks; halt democratic backsliding; cultivate cultures of lawfulness; attract investment; and tackle

violence, corruption or "strongman" regimes that use the veneer of democracy to reinforce their grip on power.[50] The Atlantic Hemisphere also offers diverse models of democratic practice that can be relevant to broader global debates about effective and responsive governance.

In many countries in the Atlantic Basin, people seeking to satisfy their basic needs are caught between corrupt elites, criminal gangs and violent extremists who offer material or other benefits. In areas with inadequate or problematic state authority, widespread poverty, and social and political marginalization, illicit economies offer livelihoods, public goods and social advancement, cultivating cultures of illegality that undermine social cohesion, economic growth and human development. Traditional rule-of-law programs that treat such activities as aberrant social activity to be suppressed or that focus solely on government institutional reform are unlikely to be sufficient. Complementary strategies are needed that seek to inculcate cultures of lawfulness in which the overwhelming majority of the population believes that the rule of law offers the best long-term path to achieving social justice, alleviate poverty and spur human development. Efforts to cultivate a culture of lawfulness in diverse regions such as Palermo, Italy, Pereira, Colombia and Monterrey, Mexico demonstrate that it is possible to initiate such a cultural change even in societies where organized crime, corruption and violence have been prevalent for decades. Atlantic countries share common interests in working to advance such efforts across the region.[51]

The Atlantic Hemisphere also offers diverse models of democratic practice that can be relevant to broader global debates about effective and responsive governance.

A shared and growing commitment to democracy, good governance and a culture of lawfulness also positions the Atlantic Hemisphere as the test bed for how established and emerging powers can formulate shared approaches to ensure the legitimacy and effectiveness of the international rules-based order. Whether emerging powers choose to challenge the current international order and its rules or promote themselves within

it depends significantly on how established democracies engage with rising democracies. The stronger the bonds among core democratic market economies, the better their chances of being able to include rising partners as responsible stakeholders in the international system.

More effective 21st century global governance is likely to depend on a more effective—and thus redefined—Atlantic Community.

The more united, integrated, interconnected and dynamic the Atlantic Hemisphere, the greater the likelihood that emerging powers will rise within this order and adhere to its rules. The looser or weaker those bonds, the greater the likelihood likelihood that emerging powers will rise within this order and adhere to its rules. The looser or weaker those bonds are, the greater the likelihood that rising powers will challenge this order. In this sense more effective 21st century global governance is likely to depend on a more effective—and thus redefined—Atlantic Community.

The Atlantic may also be a test bed of governance innovation in another sense. As this brief review has shown, traditional balance of power approaches geared to state-to-state interactions fit the Atlantic space less well than more differentiated "governance networks" that can bring together international institutions, national governments, civil society and private sector organizations in pursuit of common goals. In the Atlantic, such networks can be useful for agenda-setting and consensus-building, policy coordination, knowledge exchange, and norm-setting. The latter does not exclude or neglect competition or hard geopolitical considerations, but sets them in the broader framework of interdependence. This is all the more relevant in a context, such as the Atlantic, where relations between the main state actors are not defined predominantly in antagonistic terms and where transnational threats are largely common.[52]

The strength of Atlantic governance innovation may be to demonstrate the relevance of international non-organizations—networks that can facilitate robust functional linkages among the Atlantic continents organized around the principle of open regionalism.

If such networks are successful, then the strength of Atlantic governance innovation may be to demonstrate the relevance of international non-organizations—networks that can facilitate robust functional linkages among the Atlantic continents organized around the principle of open regionalism.[53] Open regionalism in this context means that regional efforts can help not only to address regional issues of common concern, but also to help frame broader global debates on contemporary challenges as well as appropriate norms and standards. Atlantic initiatives can have important demonstration effects, accustom officials, governments and other stakeholders to working with each other and to pioneering new ideas that can subsequently be taken up in other global fora.

WE PLEDGE TO ADVANCE OUR COOPERATION BASED ON A SHARED BELIEF IN PRINCIPLES OF DEMOCRACY, RESPECT FOR HUMAN RIGHTS AND THE RULE OF LAW, AND TO WORK TO ADVANCE THESE PRINCIPLES THROUGHOUT THE ATLANTIC REGION.

Consideration should be given to creation of an Atlantic Peer Review mechanism, a voluntary arrangement by which reform leaders consult with peers who have had personal experience with reform, drawing on experience gained from the African Peer Review Mechanism of the African Union.

- We are prepared to deploy small teams composed of our Eminent Persons, together with relevant experts, to work with reformers across the Atlantic Basin who may request such advice and counsel.

CONCLUSION

Of the world's three grand oceans, the Atlantic is the most pacific. The Pacific and Indian Oceans are tempestuous, full of rivalry and tension; the Atlantic lake, in contrast, could be a uniting force around which countries can come together.

The new dynamics of the Atlantic are not cause for neglect and indifference; they offer opportunity to test new modes of networked cooperation attuned to modern challenges. The Atlantic may offer more innovative and effective governance solutions than can be adopted within either the Asian-Pacific or Indian Ocean contexts, since traditional state-to-state mechanisms fit the Atlantic space less well than do networks of public and private actors organized around the principle of open regionalism.

The Atlantic Basin can emerge as a global laboratory and test bed for interregional, networked governance between developed and emerging countries.

Despite these trends, there are still no pan-Atlantic mechanisms comparable to Pacific Basin cooperation as embodied by APEC and other groupings. Yet as the tectonic plates of the global system continue to shift, the Atlantic Basin can emerge as a global laboratory and test bed for interregional, networked governance between developed and emerging countries— particularly if it is made clear at the outset that such efforts are not intended to contain China, compete with Pacific arrangements, or to extend Northern institutions southward. It is time to set aside zero-sum formulas of the past and to erase the invisible line dividing the South and North Atlantic by redefining a new Atlantic Community positioned to face the new world rising before us.

EMINENT PERSONS OF
THE ATLANTIC BASIN INITIATIVE

Maria Luisa P. Abrantes
Secretary of State
Member of the Board of Directors of
ANIP - Angolan National Private
Investment Agency
Angola

Geraldo Alckmin
Governor of the State of São Paulo
Brazil

Michelle Alliot-Marie
Former Minister of Foreign Affairs
Former Minister of Defense
France

Tom K. Alweendo
Director General of the National
Planning Commission
Former Governor of the Central Bank
Namibia

K.Y. Amoako
President, African Center for
Economic Transformation
Ghana

Kofi Ampim
Chairman, Societe Generale
Bank Ghana Ltd.
Chairman of Allianz Insurance
Ghana Ltd.
Ghana

Niels Annen
Member of the Bundestag
Foreign Policy Spokesman, Social
Democratic Caucus
Germany

Jose Maria Aznar
Former President of the
Government
President, FAES Foundation
Distinguished Fellow, Center for
Transatlantic Relations, Paul H.
Nitze School of Advanced
International Studies,
Johns Hopkins University
Spain

Andre Azoulay
Counselor to the King
Morocco

Gordon Bajnai
Former Prime Minister
Distinguished Fellow, Center for
Transatlantic Relations, Paul H.
Nitze School of Advanced
International Studies,
Johns Hopkins University
Hungary

Jan Peter Balkenende
Former Prime Minister
The Netherlands

Thomas Bareiss
Member of the Bundestag
Coordinator for Energy Policy, CDU/
CSU Caucus
Germany

John Bruton
Former Prime Minister
Distinguished Fellow, Center for
Transatlantic Relations, Paul H.
Nitze School of Advanced
International Studies,
Johns Hopkins University
Ireland

Jerzy Buzek
Former Prime Minister
Former President of the European
Parliament
Member of the European Parliament
Poland

Raul Diez Canseco Terry
Former Vice President of the
Republic
Founding President, Universidad San
Ignacio de Loyola
Peru

Pablo Casado
Member of Parliament
Spokesperson for European Affairs
of the Congress
Spain

Jorge Costa
Former Vice-Minister of Housing,
Public Works and Infrastructures
Member of Board of PREBUILD
Africa
Portugal

Alfredo Cotait Neto
Director of International Affairs,
Democratic Space Foundation
Brazil

Juan Jose Daboub
Former Managing Director of the
World Bank Group
Former Minister of Finance
El Salvador

Massimo D'Alema
Former Prime Minister
President, Foundation for European
Progressive Studies (FEPS) and
Fondazione Italianieuropei
Italy

Stockwell Day
Former Minister of International Trade
Former Minister of Public Safety and
Emergency Preparedness
Canada

Rut Diamint
Professor, Universidad
Torcuato Di Tella
Member of UN Advisory Board
of Disarmament Matters
Advisor, Club of Madrid
Argentina

Manuel Dias Loureiro
Former Minister of Interior
Portugal

Paula J. Dobriansky
Former Under Secretary of State for
Democracy and Global Affairs
Senior Fellow, JFK Belfer Center for
Science and International Affairs,
Harvard University
United States of America

Javier Duarte de Ochoa
Governor of the State of Veracruz
Mexico

Mikulas Dzurinda
Former Prime Minister
Former Minister of Foreign Affairs
Slovakia

Uffe Elleman Jensen
Former Minister of Foreign Affairs
Denmark

Eduardo Fernández
Former President, Christian
Democrat International
President, International Center for
Public Policy - IFEDEC
Member of the Board, Instituto de
Estudios Superiores de
Administración (IESA)
Venezuela

Leonel Fernández
Former President
Dominican Republic

Benita Ferrero-Waldner
President, EU-LAC Foundation
Former European Commissioner
for External Relations and
Neighbourhood Policy
Former European Commissioner
for Trade
Former Minister of Foreign Affairs
Austria

Franco Frattini
Justice and Chamber President,
Italian Supreme Administrative
Court
Former Minister of Foreign Affairs
Former Vice President of the
European Commission and
Commissioner for Justice,
Freedom and Liberty
Italy

Lykke Friis
Former Minister for Climate
and Energy
Former Minister for Equal Rights
Denmark

Enrique García
President & CEO, CAF –
Development Bank
of Latin America
Bolivia

Ana Maria Gomes
Member of the European Parliament
Portugal

Carlos Gomes Júnior
Former Prime Minister
of Guinea Bissau
Former President PAIGC, African
Party for the Independence of
Guinea Bissau and Cape Verde
Guinea Bissau

Ulrich Grillo
President of the Federation
of German Industries (BDI)
Germany

Dionisio Gutierrez
Chairman, Corporacion Multi
Inversiones
President, Fundación Libertad y
Desarrollo
Guatemala

Karl-Theodor zu Guttenberg
Former Minister of Defense
Former Minister of Economics
Chairman, Spitzberg Partners LLC
Germany

Daniel Hamilton
Austrian Marshall Plan Foundation
Professor
Executive Director, Center for
Transatlantic Relations
Paul H. Nitze School of Advanced
International Studies,
Johns Hopkins University
United States of America

Eveline Herfkens
Former Minister for Development
Cooperation
Founder, UN Millennium Campaign
The Netherlands

Marco Herrera
Executive Director, Fundación Global
Democracia y Desarrollo
Dominican Republic

Randy Hoback
Member of Parliament
President, ParlAmericas
Canada

Nelson Jobim
Former Minister of Defense
Former Minister of Justice
Former Chief Justice of the
Supreme Court
Brazil

James L. Jones, Jr.
(General, ret., USMC)
Former National Security Advisor to
the President of the United States
Former Supreme Allied Commander,
Europe (SACEUR)
United States of America

Donald Kaberuka
President, African Development Bank
Former Minister of Finance and
Economic Planning
Rwanda

Samuel Kame-Domguia, OCist.
Coordinator, 2050 Africa's Integrated
Maritime Strategy Task Force
African Union Commission
Ethiopia

Gilberto Kassab
Former Mayor of the
City of São Paulo
National President of PSD Social
Democratic Party
Brazil

Colin Kenny
Senator
Canada

Hans-Ulrich Klose
Former Chairman of the Foreign
Affairs Committee of the
Bundestag
Former First Mayor of Hamburg
Germany

Bernard Kouchner
Former Minister of Foreign Affairs
Co-Founder of Médecins Sans
Frontières and Médecins du
Monde
France

Pedro Pablo Kuczynski
Former Prime Minister
Peru

Luis Alberto LaCalle
Former President
Uruguay

Jean-David Levitte
Former Diplomatic Advisor and
Sherpa to the President of France
Former Ambassador to the United
States
France

Jane Holl Lute
President and CEO, Council on
Cybersecurity
Former Deputy Secretary of
Homeland Security
United States of America

Mauricio Macri
Mayor, City of Buenos Aires
Argentina

Guilherme F. Mattar
Former São Paulo City Secretary
for International Relations
Brazil

Vicente Lopez-Ibor Mayor
Former Energy Commissioner
President, Estudio Juridico
International
Spain

Greg Mills
Director, Brenthurst Foundation
South Africa

Marcilio Marques Moreira
Former Minister of the Economy,
Finance and Planning
Former Ambassador to the United
States
Brazil

Pedro Mouriño Uzal
Chairman & CEO Mediasiete S.A.
Spain

Felix Mutati
Member of Parliament
Former Minister of Commerce
Zambia

Aécio Neves da Cunha
Senator
Former Governor of Minas Gerais
Brazil

Olusegun Obasanjo
Former President
Nigeria

Joao Benedict Okey Oramah
Executive Vice President
    African Export-Import Bank
Nigeria

Marcelino Oreja Arburúa
CEO, Enagás, S.A.
Spain

Richard Ottaway
Member of Parliament and
    Chairman of the Foreign Affairs
    Committee
United Kingdom

Ana Palacio
Former Senior Vice President and
    General Counsel of the World
    Bank Group
Former Minister of Foreign Affairs
Spain

Jean Ping
Former President of the United
    Nations General Assembly
Former Chair of the African Union
    Commission
Former Minister of Foreign Affairs
Gabon

Josep Piqué
Former Minister of Foreign Affairs
Former Minister of Industry
Spain

Balbino Prieto
President, Spanish Exporters &
    Investors Club
Vice-President, CITHA - European
    Confederation of International
    Trading Houses
Spain

Jorge Quiroga
Former President of the Republic
Vice President, Club of Madrid
Bolivia

Miguel Relvas
Former Minister of Parliamentary
    Affairs
Portugal

Bill Richardson
Former Governor of New Mexico
Former Secretary of Energy
Former Ambassador to the United
    Nations
United States of America

Miguel Ángel Rodríguez Echeverría
Former President of the Republic
Former Secretary General of the
    Organization of American
    States (OAS)
Costa Rica

Norbert Röttgen
Chairman, Foreign Affairs
    Committee of the Bundestag
Former Minister for Environment,
    Nature Protection and Reactor
    Safety
Germany

Abel Rwendeire
Chair, National Planning Authority
Former Minister of State for Higher
    Education
Former Minister of State for
    Trade and Industry
Uganda

Roberto Saba
Dean and Professor of Constitutional
    Law and Human Rights
    Palermo University School of Law,
    Buenos Aires
Argentina

Francisco Salazar
Chair, Energy Regulatory
    Commission (CRE)
Chair of the Iberoamerican
    Association of Energy
    Regulators (ARIAE)
Mexico

Piero Scarpellini
Former chief of staff to the Prime
    Minister of Italy and President of
    the European Commission
Former General Director, Pragmata
    Institute
Republic of San Marino

Mamadou Seck
Former President of the National
    Assembly
Former Mayor of the Municipality
    of Mbao
Senegal

Anne-Marie Slaughter
President and CEO, New America
    Foundation
Former Director of Policy Planning,
    U.S. Department of State
Former Dean, Woodrow Wilson
    School of Public and International
    Affairs, Princeton University
United States of America

Clifford Sobel
Former Ambassador to Brazil
Former Ambassador to the
    Netherlands
United States of America

Rodrigo Tavares
Head of the São Paulo State's
    Government Office of
    Foreign Affairs
Brazil

Jean-Claude Thebault
Director-General, Bureau of
    European Policy Advisors
    European Commission
France

Mauricio Toledano
CEO, Grupo Eurofinsa
Spain

Max Trejo
Assistant Secretary General
    Ibero-American Youth Organization
Mexico

Žiga Turk
Former Minister for Growth
Former Minister for Education,
    Science, Culture and Sports
Former Secretary General of the
    Reflection Group on the Future
    of Europe
Slovenia

Alvaro Uribe Vélez
Former President
Colombia

Alfredo Valladão
Professor, Sciences Po, Paris
President, Advisory Board,
    EU-Brazil Association
Brazil

Günter Verheugen
Former European Commissioner
    for Enlargement
Former European Commissioner
    for Enterprise and Industry
Germany

Vaira Vīķe-Freiberga
Former President of the Republic
President, Club of Madrid
Latvia

Paul Wolfowitz
Former President of the World Bank
Former Deputy Secretary of Defense
Former Dean, Paul H. Nitze School
    of Advanced International Studies,
    Johns Hopkins University
United States of America

Eduardo Zaplana
Director for Institutional Affairs,
    Telefonica
Former Minister of Labor
Spain

Ernesto Zedillo
Former President
Director, Center for the Study of
    Globalization, Yale University
Mexico

These Eminent Persons endorse the general policy thrust and judgments set forth in this document, though not necessarily every finding and recommendation. They participate in the Atlantic Basin Initiative in their individual, not institutional, capacities. The views expressed here do not necessarily reflect the views of any government or institution.

The Eminent Persons network of the Atlantic Basin Initiative continues to grow. The evolving list is available at transatlantic.sais-jhu.edu.

We wish to thank the following individuals who have joined in Atlantic Basin deliberations.

Roberto Abdenur
Former Ambassador to the United States, Germany, and China
Brazil

Amado Philip de Andrés
United Nations Office on Drugs and Crime (UNODC)

Assunção dos Anjos
Former Minister of Foreign Affairs
Angola

Fareed Arthur
African Union Commission
Ghana

Rafael L. Bardaji
Foreign Policy Director, FAES Foundation
Former National Security Advisor
Spain

Michaela Biancofiore
Member of Parliament; Deputy Speaker for Foreign Affairs
Italy

Tendai Biti
Movement for Democratic Change
Zimbabwe

José Ramon Brea
CEO, IBT Group
Dominican Republic

Nancy Brune
Senior Policy Analyst, Sandia National Laboratories
United States of America

Kevin Casas-Zamora
Secretary for Political Affairs, Organization of American States (OAS)
Costa Rica

Margarita Cedeño de Fernández
Vice President
Dominican Republic

Laurence Cockroft
Co-Founder, Transparency International
United Kingdom

Luisa Dias Diogo
Former Prime Minister
Mozambique

Charles Doran
Andrew W. Mellon Professor of International Relations,
Paul H. Nitze School of Advanced International Studies,
Johns Hopkins University
United States of America

Charlie Edwards
Director of National Security and Resilience Studies, Royal United Services Institute
United Kingdom

Jean-Louis Ekra
Chairman and President, African Export-Import Bank
Côte d'Ivoire

Stephen Ellis
Desmond Tutu Professor, Vrije Universiteit Amsterdam
Senior Researcher, Afrika Studiecentrum Leiden
The Netherlands

Tony O. Elumelu, CON
Chairman, Heirs Holdings Ltd.
Founder of The Tony Elumelu Foundation
Nigeria

Antoni Estevadeordal
Manager, Integration and Trade Sector
Inter-American Development Bank
Spain

Deborah Farias
University of British Columbia
Canada/Brazil

Vanda Felbab-Brown
Senior Fellow, the Brookings Institution
United States of America

Malcolm Ferguson
Former Ambassador to Mexico
South Africa

Renato Flores
Professor, Fundação Getulio Vargas
Brazil

João Fonseca
CEO of Lagoon International
Portugal

Roy Godson
President, National Strategy Information Center
United States of America

Armando Marques Guedes
Professor of Law, Universidade Nova de Lisboa
Portugal

Wibke Hansen
Deputy Director and Head of Analysis, Center for International Peace Operations (ZIF)
Germany

Jorge Heine
CIGI Distinguished Fellow and Chair of Global Governance
Balsillie School of International Affairs, Wilfrid Laurier University
Former Ambassador of Chile to India, Bangladesh and Sri Lanka
Canada/Chile

Jeffrey Herbst
President
Colgate University
United States of America

Paul Isbell
Senior Fellow, Center for Transatlantic Relations,
Paul H. Nitze School of Advanced International Studies,
Johns Hopkins University
United States of America

Martin Kimani
Permanent Representative and Head of Mission to the United Nations in Nairobi
Kenya

Francis Kornegay
Senior Research Fellow
Institute for Global Dialogue, Pretoria
United States of America/ South Africa

Winrich Kühne
Center for International Peace Operations (ZIF)
Steven Muller Professor,
Paul H. Nitze School of Advanced International Studies,
Johns Hopkins University
Germany

Laurent Salvador Lamothe
Prime Minister
Haiti

Terence McNamee
Deputy Director
    Brenthurst Foundation
South Africa

Tito Mendoça
CEO of Erigo
Angola

Philipp Mißfelder
Member of the Bundestag
Coordinator of Transatlantic
    Cooperation, Federal
    Foreign Office
Germany

Luis Alberto Moreno
President, Inter-American
    Development Bank
Colombia

Enrique Navarro
CEO, IC2 Partners
Spain

Mumba Nevers
Movement for Multiparty Democracy
Zambia

Frank Nweke
Director General, Nigerian Economic
    Summit Group
Nigeria

Joseph Nyagah
Former Minister of Cooperative
    Development and Marketing
Kenya

Anthony Okkara
Director of Cabinet, Deputy
    Chairman of the African Union
Kenya

Jonathan Oppenheimer
E Oppenheimer & Son
South Africa

Nicky Oppenheimer
E Oppenheimer & Son
South Africa

Michael Penfold
Director of Public Policies and
    Competitiveness
    CAF Development Bank
Venezuela

Nicky Prins
Chief Director, National Treasury
South Africa

Joseph Quinlan
Senior Fellow, Center for
    Transatlantic Relations,
    Paul H. Nitze School of Advanced
    International Studies,
    Johns Hopkins University
United States of America

Dan Restrepo
Former Special Assistant to the
    President and Senior Director for
    Western Hemisphere
    Affairs,National Security Staff
United States of America

Antonio Rodríguez-Pina
President, Deutsche Bank
Spain

Riordan Roett
Professor and Director of the Latin
    American Studies Program and
    Western Hemisphere Studies
    Paul H. Nitze School of Advanced
    International Studies,
    Johns Hopkins University
United States of America

Lorena Ruano
Jean Monnet Chair, División de
    Estudios Internacionales,
    Centro de Investigación y
    Docencia Económicas (CIDE)
Mexico

Vanessa Rubio Márquez
Undersecretary of Foreign Affairs for
    Latin America and the Caribbean
Mexico

Andras Simonyi
Managing Director, Center for
    Transatlantic Relations,
    Paul H. Nitze School of Advanced
    International Studies,
    Johns Hopkins University
Former Ambassador to the
    United States
Hungary

Rachel Slack
E Oppenheimer & Son
South Africa

Mike Spicer
CEO, Business Leadership SA
South Africa

Steve Thorne
Director, South South North
South Africa

Augusto Tomas
Minister of Transportation
Angola

Martin Uadiale
Department of International Studies
    and Diplomacy, Benson Idahosa
    University
Nigeria

Roel van der Veen
Academic Advisor, Ministry of
    Foreign Affairs
The Netherlands

Jordi Vaquer Fanés
Open Society Initiative for Europe
Spain

Juan Carlos De La Hoz Vinas
Head of Operations, Representative
    Office in Brazil
    Inter-American Development
    Bank
Brazil

Manuel Vicente
Vice President
Angola

Judith Vorrath
Associate, German Institute for
International and Security Affairs
    (SWP)
Germany

Phil Williams
Wesley Posvar Professor of
    International Relations, University
    of Pittsburgh
United States of America

Oscar Iván Zuluaga
Former Minister of Finance
Colombia

NOTES

1. For background see Álvaro de Vasconcelos, ed. *Global Trends 2030 - Citizens in an Interconnected and Polycentric World*. Paris: EU Institute for Security Studies, 2012; http://www.waterencyclopedia.com/Mi-Oc/Ocean-Basins.html#ixzz2BphFo6Cr; Daniel S. Hamilton and Joseph P. Quinlan, *The Transatlantic Economy 2014*. Washington, DC: Center for Transatlantic Relations, 2014; http://www.encyclopedia.com/topic/Atlantic_Ocean.aspx#4; http://www.wordiq.com/definition/Atlantic_Ocean; http://www.encyclopedia.com/topic/Atlantic_Ocean.aspx#3.

2. See Amy Myers Jafee, "The Americas, not the Middle East, will be the World Capital of Energy." *Foreign Policy*, Sept/Oct 2011; Paul Isbell, *Energy and the Atlantic. The Shifting Energy Landscape of the Atlantic Basin*. Washington, DC: German Marshall Fund of the United States, 2012.

3. Ibid.

4. See U.S. Energy Information Administration; Steven Mufson, "Shale gas reshaping the U.S. industrial landscape," *The Washington Post*, November 15, 2012; http://news.yahoo.com/u-overtake-saudi-top-oil-producer-iea-132331660.html; National Energy Board, "Energy Facts," July 2011; http://www.canadasenergy.ca/wp-content/uploads/2012/08/Final-Document-Aug-1.pdf , p. 120; Tom Fowler, "After spill, gulf oil drilling rebounds." *The Wall Street Journal*, September 21, 2012, p. B1; http://www.bizjournals.com/houston/print-edition/2013/03/01/drilling-in-the-gulf-risk-and-reward.html; http://www.ihs.com/products/oil-gas-information/drilling-data/weekly-rig-count.aspx.

5. Jaffe, op. cit.; Isbell, op. cit.; Pierre-René Bauquis, "What the future for extra heavy oil and bitumen: the Orinoco case", February 16, 2006. World Energy Council, http://web.archive.org/web/20070402100135/http://www.worldenergy.org/wec-geis/publications/default/tech_papers/17th_congress/3_1_04.asp; http://www.worldfolio.co.uk/region/south-america/colombia/enertotal-colombia-n1721#sthash.8cWTJRwk.dpuf; http://articles.washingtonpost.com/2012-05-25/world/35455218_1_oil-and-gas-oil-powers-barrels; http://www.rand.org/content/dam/rand/pubs/technical_reports/2012/RAND_TR1144z4.pdf.

6. http://www.canadasenergy.ca/wp-content/uploads/2012/08/Final-Document-Aug-1.pdf, p. 124; http://seekingalpha.com/article/1202741-u-s-lng-exports-increasingly-a-reality; Steven Mufson, "Turning the tankers around," *The Washington Post*, December 9, 2012, p. G1; http://www.deloitte.com/assets/Dcom-UnitedStates/Local%20Assets/Documents/Energy_us_er/us_er_GlobalImpactUSLNGExports_AmericanRenaissance_Jan2013.pdf; http://www.oxfordenergy.org/wpcms/wp-content/uploads/2012/10/NG-68.pdf

7. Isbell, op. cit.

8. Isbell, op. cit.

9. See Jean Kowal, 'Medgrid Objectives and Approach," http://www.medgrid-psm.com/wp-content/uploads/2013/12/Medgrid-Objectives-and-approach-JEAN-KOWAL.pdf; Isabelle Werenfels and Kirsten Westphal, „Solarstrom aus Nordafrika: Rahmenbedingungen und Perspektiven," *SWP-Studie*, Februar 2010 (Berlin: Stiftung Wissenschaft und Politik, 2010); Daniel Schäfer, „Solarthermie, Physik und Technik der Solarthermie in Afrika," *Spiegel der Forschung*, 2, December 2008, pp. 11-15, available at http://geb.uni-giessen.de/geb/volltexte/2009/6731/pdf/SdF_2008-02-11-15.pdf>.

10. These include, among others, the World Bank's Clean Technology Fund, Strategic Climate Fund, Scaling Up Renewable Energy Program in Low Income Countries, the UNDP's UN-REDD Programme, and the various funds of the Global Environment Facility. For more, see http://www.climatefundsupdate.org/.

11. In 2009, more than 1.45 million African lives were lost to household pollution caused by inefficient biomass cooking stoves. Fewer people died from malaria. http://oilprice.com/Energy/Energy-General/Solving-Energy-Poverty-in-Sub-Saharan-Africa.html; Isbell, op. cit.

12. International Energy Agency (IEA)D. *Energy for All: financing access for the poor*. Paris, 2011; http://www.forbes.com/sites/blakeclayton/2012/11/09/the-biggest-energy-problem-that-rarely-makes-headlines/; International Energy Agency, *World Energy Outlook 2010*, Paris, 2010.

13. Isbell, op. cit.

14. P. Collier and A. Venables, 2007. "Rethinking Trade Preferences: How Africa Can Diversify its Exports," *The World Economy*, 30(8): 1326-45.

15. Lorena Ruano, "Merchandise Trade in the Atlantic Basin, 2000-2012," in Daniel S. Hamilton, ed., *Atlantic Rising: Changing Commercial Dynamics in the Atlantic Basin*. Washington, DC: Center for Transatlantic Relations, 2014.

16. Robert D. Kaplan, *The Revenge of Geography*. New York: Random House 2012, p. 333.

17. Hamilton/Quinlan, op. cit.

18. Daniel S. Hamilton and Joseph P. Quinlan, "Commercial Ties in the Atlantic Basin: The Evolving Role of Services and Investment," in *Atlantic Rising*, op. cit.

19. Ibid.

20. http://edition.cnn.com/2012/06/07/business/brazil-africa-business/index.html.

21. While the services sector accounts for only 23% of global exports, it accounts for over 70% of GDP in advanced economies. Martin Wolf, *Why Globalization Works*. New Haven: Yale University Press, 2004.

22. The gains stemming from the liberalization of services could potentially be larger than in all other areas of international trade.

23. Eurostat.

24. Daniel Hamilton, *Europe 2020 -- Competitive or Complacent?* Washington, DC.: Center for Transatlantic Relations, 2011.

25. Even in resource-rich economies in Africa services between 1999 and 2008 came to account for over 40 percent of GDP, more than industry. See Uri Dardush and William Shaw, *Juggernaut - How Emerging Markets are Shaping Globlization*. Washington DC Carnegie Endowment for International Peace, 2012, p. 186.; http://www.economywatch.com/world_economy/brazil/structure-of-economy.html.

26. Ecorys, Deltares, Oecanic, 2012. *Blue Growth. Scenarios and drivers for Sustainable Growth from the Oceans, Seas and Coasts*. Final Report. Study on behalf of the European Commission, DG MARE. https://webgate.ec.europa.eu/maritimeforum/content/2946; http://ec.europa.eu/maritimeaffairs/policy/blue_growth/documents/com_2012_494_en.pdf

27. Eveline Herfkens, "Harmonized Trade Preferences for Low Income African Countries: A Transatlantic Initiative," in Daniel S. Hamilton, *Atlantic Rising*, op. cit.; Also K.Y. Amaoko, Daniel Hamilton and Eveline Herfkens, "A Transatlantic Deal for Africa," *New York Times*, May 8, 2013, available at http://www.nytimes.com/2013/05/08/opinion/global/A-Trans-Atlantic-Deal-for-Africa.html?_r=0

28. Robert Zoellick, "Five questions for the world's next trade chief," *Financial Times*, April 2, 2013.

29. http://www.encyclopedia.com/topic/Atlantic_Ocean.aspx#2; http://library.thinkquest.org/06aug/00051/Mareks%20page.html.

30. C. Nellemann, S. Hain, and J. Alder, (eds), *In Dead Water – Merging of climate change with pollution, over-harvest, and infestations in the world's fishing grounds*. United Nations Environment Programme, GRID-Arendal, Norway, February 2008; http://www.pik-potsdam.de/~stefan/Publications/Book_chapters/rahmstorf_eqs_2006.pdf; http://mgg.rsmas.miami.edu/groups/sil/submission.pdf.

31. Asbury H. Sallenger, Kara S. Doran and Peter A. Howd, ''Hotspot of accelerated sea-level rise on the Atlantic coast of North America," *Nature Climate Change 2*, 884–888 (2012), 24 June 2012. doi:10.1038/nclimate1597.

32. http://www.nature.com/nclimate/journal/v2/n12/full/nclimate1597.html. In the U.S. sea levels have been rising faster than the global average along the eastern coast for the past 60 years. Boston, Atlantic City, Norfolk and Charleston had 3 times the average number of storm surge tides during that period. Dutch climate models predict that the North Sea will rise about 16 inches by 2050 and up to 13 feet by 2200. Robert Lee Hotz, "Keeping Our Heads Above Water," *The Wall Street Journal*, December 1-2, 2012.

1. For background see Álvaro de Vasconcelos, ed. *Global Trends 2030 - Citizens in an Interconnected and Polycentric World*. Paris: EU Institute for Security Studies, 2012; http://www.waterencyclopedia.com/Mi-Oc/Ocean-Basins.html#ixzz2BphFo6Cr; Daniel S. Hamilton and Joseph P. Quinlan, *The Transatlantic Economy 2014*. Washington, DC: Center for Transatlantic Relations, 2014; http://www.encyclopedia.com/topic/Atlantic_Ocean.aspx#4; http://www.wordiq.com/definition/Atlantic_Ocean; http://www.encyclopedia.com/topic/Atlantic_Ocean.aspx#3.

2. See Amy Myers Jafee, "The Americas, not the Middle East, will be the World Capital of Energy." *Foreign Policy*, Sept/Oct 2011; Paul Isbell, *Energy and the Atlantic. The Shifting Energy Landscape of the Atlantic Basin*. Washington, DC: German Marshall Fund of the United States, 2012.

3. Ibid.

4. See U.S. Energy Information Administration; Steven Mufson, "Shale gas reshaping the U.S. industrial landscape," *The Washington Post*, November 15, 2012; http://news.yahoo.com/u-overtake-saudi-top-oil-producer-iea-132331660.html; National Energy Board, "Energy Facts," July 2011; http://www.canadasenergy.ca/wp-content/uploads/2012/08/Final-Document-Aug-1.pdf , p. 120; Tom Fowler, "After spill, gulf oil drilling rebounds." *The Wall Street Journal*, September 21, 2012, p. B1; http://www.bizjournals.com/houston/print-edition/2013/03/01/drilling-in-the-gulf-risk-and-reward.html; http://www.ihs.com/products/oil-gas-information/drilling-data/weekly-rig-count.aspx.

5. Jaffe, op. cit.; Isbell, op. cit.; Pierre-René Bauquis, "What the future for extra heavy oil and bitumen: the Orinoco case", February 16, 2006. World Energy Council, http://web.archive.org/web/20070402100135/http://www.worldenergy.org/wec-geis/publications/default/tech_papers/17th_congress/3_1_04.asp; http://www.worldfolio.co.uk/region/south-america/colombia/enertotal-colombia-n1721#sthash.8cWTJRwk.dpuf; http://articles.washingtonpost.com/2012-05-25/world/35455218_1_oil-and-gas-oil-powers-barrels; http://www.rand.org/content/dam/rand/pubs/technical_reports/2012/RAND_TR1144z4.pdf.

6. http://www.canadasenergy.ca/wp-content/uploads/2012/08/Final-Document-Aug-1.pdf, p. 124; http://seekingalpha.com/article/1202741-u-s-lng-exports-increasingly-a-reality; Steven Mufson, "Turning the tankers around," *The Washington Post*, December 9, 2012, p. G1; http://www.deloitte.com/assets/Dcom-UnitedStates/Local%20Assets/Documents/Energy_us_er/us_er_GlobalImpactUSLNGExports_AmericanRenaissance_Jan2013.pdf; http://www.oxfordenergy.org/wpcms/wp-content/uploads/2012/10/NG-68.pdf

7. Isbell, op. cit.

8. Isbell, op. cit.

9. See Jean Kowal, 'Medgrid Objectives and Approach," http://www.medgrid-psm.com/wp-content/uploads/2013/12/Medgrid-Objectives-and-approach-JEAN-KOWAL.pdf; Isabelle Werenfels and Kirsten Westphal, „Solarstrom aus Nordafrika: Rahmenbedingungen und Perspektiven," *SWP-Studie*, Februar 2010 (Berlin: Stiftung Wissenschaft und Politik, 2010); Daniel Schäfer, „Solarthermie, Physik und Technik der Solarthermie in Afrika," *Spiegel der Forschung*, 2, December 2008, pp. 11-15, available at http://geb.uni-giessen.de/geb/volltexte/2009/6731/pdf/SdF_2008-02-11.15.pdf>.

10. These include, among others, the World Bank's Clean Technology Fund, Strategic Climate Fund, Scaling Up Renewable Energy Program in Low Income Countries, the UNDP's UN-REDD Programme, and the various funds of the Global Environment Facility. For more, see http://www.climatefundsupdate.org/.

11. In 2009, more than 1.45 million African lives were lost to household pollution caused by inefficient biomass cooking stoves. Fewer people died from malaria. http://oilprice.com/Energy/Energy-General/Solving-Energy-Poverty-in-Sub-Saharan-Africa.html; Isbell, op cit.

12. International Energy Agency (IEA)D. *Energy for All: financing access for the poor*. Paris, 2011; http://www.forbes.com/sites/blakeclayton/2012/11/09/the-biggest-energy-problem-that-rarely-makes-headlines/; International Energy Agency, *World Energy Outlook 2010*, Paris, 2010.

13. Isbell, op. cit.

14. P. Collier and A. Venables, 2007. "Rethinking Trade Preferences: How Africa Can Diversify its Exports," *The World Economy*, 30(8): 1326-45.

15. Lorena Ruano, "Merchandise Trade in the Atlantic Basin, 2000-2012," in Daniel S. Hamilton, ed., *Atlantic Rising: Changing Commercial Dynamics in the Atlantic Basin*. Washington, DC: Center for Transatlantic Relations, 2014.

16. Robert D. Kaplan, *The Revenge of Geography*. New York: Random House 2012, p. 333.

17. Hamilton/Quinlan, op. cit.

18. Daniel S. Hamilton and Joseph P. Quinlan, "Commercial Ties in the Atlantic Basin: The Evolving Role of Services and Investment," in *Atlantic Rising*, op. cit.

19. Ibid.

20. http://edition.cnn.com/2012/06/07/business/brazil-africa-business/index.html.

21. While the services sector accounts for only 23% of global exports, it accounts for over 70% of GDP in advanced economies. Martin Wolf, *Why Globalization Works*. New Haven: Yale University Press, 2004.

22. The gains stemming from the liberalization of services could potentially be larger than in all other areas of international trade.

23. Eurostat.

24. Daniel Hamilton, *Europe 2020 -- Competitive or Complacent?* Washington, DC.: Center for Transatlantic Relations, 2011.

25. Even in resource-rich economies in Africa services between 1999 and 2008 came to account for over 40 percent of GDP, more than industry. See Uri Dardush and William Shaw, *Juggernaut - How Emerging Markets are Shaping Globlization*. Washington DC Carnegie Endowment for International Peace, 2012, p. 186.; http://www.economywatch.com/world_economy/brazil/structure-of-economy.html.

26. Ecorys, Deltares, Oecanic, 2012. *Blue Growth. Scenarios and drivers for Sustainable Growth from the Oceans, Seas and Coasts*. Final Report. Study on behalf of the European Commission, DG MARE. https://webgate.ec.europa.eu/maritimeforum/content/2946; http://ec.europa.eu/maritimeaffairs/policy/blue_growth/documents/com_2012_494_en.pdf

27. Eveline Herfkens, "Harmonized Trade Preferences for Low Income African Countries: A Transatlantic Initiative," in Daniel S. Hamilton, *Atlantic Rising*, op. cit.; Also K.Y. Amaoko, Daniel Hamilton and Eveline Herfkens, "A Transatlantic Deal for Africa," *New York Times*, May 8, 2013, available at http://www.nytimes.com/2013/05/08/opinion/global/A-Trans-Atlantic-Deal-for-Africa.html?_r=0

28. Robert Zoellick, "Five questions for the world's next trade chief," *Financial Times*, April 2, 2013.

29. http://www.encyclopedia.com/topic/Atlantic_Ocean.aspx#2; http://library.thinkquest.org/06aug/00051/Mareks%20page.html.

30. C. Nellemann, S. Hain, and J. Alder, (eds), *In Dead Water – Merging of climate change with pollution, over-harvest, and infestations in the world's fishing grounds*. United Nations Environment Programme, GRID-Arendal, Norway, February 2008; http://www.pik-potsdam.de/~stefan/Publications/Book_chapters/rahmstorf_eqs_2006.pdf; http://mgg.rsmas.miami.edu/groups/sil/submission.pdf.

31. Asbury H. Sallenger, Kara S. Doran and Peter A. Howd, "Hotspot of accelerated sea-level rise on the Atlantic coast of North America," *Nature Climate Change 2*, 884–888 (2012), 24 June 2012. doi:10.1038/nclimate1597.

32. http://www.nature.com/nclimate/journal/v2/n12/full/nclimate1597.html. In the U.S. sea levels have been rising faster than the global average along the eastern coast for the past 60 years. Boston, Atlantic City, Norfolk and Charleston had 3 times the average number of storm surge tides during that period. Dutch climate models predict that the North Sea will rise about 16 inches by 2050 and up to 13 feet by 2200. Robert Lee Hotz, "Keeping Our Heads Above Water," *The Wall Street Journal*, December 1-2, 2012.

33. http://www.whitehouse.gov/sites/default/files/microsites/ostp/hypoxia-report.pdf; Robert J. Diaz and Rutger Rosenberg, "Spreading Dead Zones and Consequences for Marine Ecosystems," *Science*, Vol. 321 no. 5891, pp. 926-929, August 15, 2008; DOI: 10.1126/science.1156401; (Table 1 and Appendix III); http://www.sciencemag.org/content/321/5891/926.abstract; Diaz and Rosenberg, op. cit.; NASA Earth Observatory; http://www.fishupdate.com/news/fullstory.php/aid/14724/__Dead_zone_growing_in_Atlantic;_billfish_affected.html; http://www.whitehouse.gov/sites/default/files/microsites/ostp/hypoxia-report.pdf.

34. Richardson, John, et al. *The Fractured Ocean. Current Challenges to Maritime Policy in the Wider Atlantic*. Washington, DC: German Marshall Fund of the United States/OCP Foundation, 2012.

35. Watson R.; Pauly D. "Systematic distortion in world fisheries catch trends." *Nature*. 2001;424:534–536.

36. Richardson, op. cit.; http://www.earthgauge.net/wp-content/CF_Atlantic.pdf

37. Ibid.

38. Ibid.

39. Ecorys et al, 2012DOI:.

40. Ian Lesser, et al. *Morocco's New Geopolitics*. Washington, DC: German Marshall Fund of the United States/OCP Foundation, 2012.

41. http://www.thisisafrica.me/opinion/detail/19586/the-growing-problem-of-illegal-drugs-in-africa; http://www.unodc.org/westandcentralafrica/en/cape-verde.html; Department of State '2012 International Narcotics Control Strategy Report (INSCR)', http://www.state.gov/j/inl/rls/nrcrpt/2012/vol1/184100.htm#Kenya; http://www.irinnews.org/report/81910/liberia-drug-abuse-on-the-rise; Department of State '2012 International Narcotics Control Strategy Report (INSCR)', http://www.state.gov/j/inl/rls/nrcrpt/2012/vol1/184102.htm#Tanzania; http://allafrica.com/stories/201301151322.html; Department of State '2012 International Narcotics Control Strategy Report (INSCR)', http://www.state.gov/j/inl/rls/nrcrpt/2012/vol1/184102.htm#South_Africa; http://www.npr.org/2013/01/01/168072712/brazils-drug-epidemic-welcome-to-crackland; http://www.economist.com/news/americas/21575810-worlds-biggest-crack-market-seeks-better-way-deal-addicts-cracking-up; General Secretariat of the Organization of American States (OAS), *The Drug Problem in the Americas*, OEA/Ser.D/XXV.4, 2013.

42. Ibid.

43. Global Financial Integrity, *Illicit Financial Flows from Developing Countries 2001-10*. Figures are derived from IMF figures on Direction of Trade and Balance of Payments. True numbers are difficult to ascertain, but there is no doubt that flows are substantial.

44. See Phil Williams, "Illicit Flows and Networks in the Atlantic Basin," in Daniel S. Hamilton, ed., *Dark Networks in the Atlantic Basin: Emerging Trends and Implications for Human Security*. Washington, DC: Center for Transatlantic Relations, 2014.

45. Kwesi Aning, *Security Links between Trafficking and Terrorism in the Sahel in Africa South of the Sahara*. London: Routledge, 2011; Terje Østebø, "Islamic Militancy in Africa," *African Security Brief*, No. 23, November 2012, Africa Center for Strategic Studies. http://africacenter.org/wp content/uploads/2012/11/AfricaBriefFinal_23.pdf; Wolfram Lacher, "Organized Crime and Conflict in the Sahel-Sahara Region." Washington, DC: Carnegie Endowment for International Peace, September 2012.

46. Charles and Clifford Kupchan, "Concerts, Collective Security, and the Future of Europe," *International Security*, 16,1, pp. 118; Both Robert Kaplan and Jonathan Holslag suggest that new maritime concerts may be applicable to the Pacific and Indian Oceans. See Robert Kaplan, *Monsoon: The Indian Ocean and the Future of American Power*. New York: Random House, 2010; Robert D. Kaplan, *The Revenge of Geography*. New York: Random House, 2012; and Jonathan Holslag, "Crowded, Connected and Contested." http://www.eu-asiacentre.eu/pub_details.php?pub_id=71. Yet on balance the Atlantic seems a more propitious place to start.

47. For concrete examples where such transfer of lessons could be useful see David O'Reagan, *Cocaine and Instability in Africa: Lessons from Latin America and the Caribbean*, Africa Security Brief No. 5, July 2010.

48. IBM Global Business Services, "Global Movement Management: Commerce, Security, and Resilience in Today's Networked World," and "Global Movement Management: Securing the Global Economy," available through www.ibm.com/gbs/government. For more on the international aspects of resilient networks, see Bengt Sundelius, "Beyond Anti-Terrorism: Ensuring Free and Resilient Societies," in Daniel S. Hamilton, ed., *Shoulder to Shoulder: Forging a Strategic U.S.-EU Partnership* (Washington, DC: Center for Transatlantic Relations, 2010); Esther Brimmer and Daniel S. Hamilton, "Introduction: Five Dimensions of Homeland and International Security," in Esther Brimmer, ed., *Five Dimensions of Homeland and International Security* (Washington, DC: Center for Transatlantic Relations, 2008);

49. Latin America has moved from authoritarianism to democracy; closed markets to open markets; and from import substitution to export-orientation. Juan Gabriel Tolkatlian, "A View from Latin America," in Riordan Roett and Guadalupe Paz, eds., *China's Expansion into the Western Hemisphere. Implications for Latin America and the United States*. Washington DC: Brookings 2008. p. 64.

50. See Charles Kupchan, *No One's World*. Oxford University Press, 2012.

51. As Kwesi Aning and John Pokoo note: "Recent seizures and arrests in several West African countries have shed light on how the work of trafficking networks is facilitated by a range of actors, including businessmen, politicians, members of the security forces and the judiciary, clergymen, traditional leaders and youth." Kwesi Aning and John Pokoo, *Drug Trafficking And Threats to National and Regional Security in West Africa*, West Africa Commission on Drugs Background Paper No. 1, 2013, p. 5. For more on building a culture of lawfulness, see National Strategy Information Center, "Building a Culture of Lawfulness: A Guide to Getting Started" (Washington, DC, 2011), http://www.strategycenter.org/wp-content/uploads/2012/03/World_Bank_Report.pdf; National Strategy Information Center, *Fostering A Culture of Lawfulness: Multi-Sector Success in Pereira, Colombia* (Washington, DC, 2010), http://www.strategycenter.org/wp-content/uploads/2011/03/Fostering-a-Culture-of-Lawfulness.pdf.; Roy Godson, "Guide to Developing a Culture of Lawfulness." Paper presented at the Symposium on the Role of Civil Society in Countering Organized Crime: Global Implications of the Palermo, Sicily Renaissance. Palermo, Italy. December 14, 2000; Vanda Felbab-Brown, "Designing Pan-Atlantic and International Anti-Crime Cooperation," in *Dark Networks in the Atlantic Basin*, op. cit.

52. de Vasconcelos, op. cit., pp. 240, 263; Joseph S. Nye, *The Future of Power*. New York: Public Affairs, 2011, p. 216; Daniel Hamilton and Kurt Volker, eds. *Transatlantic 2020: A Tale of Four Futures*. Washington, DC: Center for Transatlantic Relations, 2011; G. John Ikenberry, "The Future of the Liberal World Order," *Foreign Affairs*, May/June 2011.

53. C. Fred Bergsten, "Open Regionalism," *Working Paper 97-3*, Institute for International Economics. Washington, DC, 1997.